TABLE OF CONTENTS

ACRONYMS

C4ISR	Command, Control, Communications, Computers, Intelligence, Surveillance, and Reconnaissance
BICI	Bahraini Independent Commission of Inquiry
GCC	Gulf Cooperation Council
KSA	Kingdom of Saudi Arabia
MBT	Main Battle Tank
PSF	Peninsula Shield Force
R-DIME	Religion, Diplomatic, Information, Military, and Economic Instruments of Power
Sunni	Sunni Sect of Islam or Sunni followers of Islam
Shia	Shia Sect of Islam or Shia followers of Islam
UAE	United Arab Emirates
UN	United Nations

TABLES

CHAPTER 1

INTRODUCTION

On the 14th of March 2011, as violent anti-government protests continued to escalate after three weeks on the small island kingdom of Bahrain, a substantial foreign troop presence entered the country from the east, crossing over the King Fahd Causeway in order to "help protect the safety of citizens, residents and critical infrastructure."[1] The foreign troops, actually Saudi Arabian and United Arab Emirati, were part of the Peninsula Shield Force (PSF), the military wing of the Gulf Cooperative Council (GCC). The PSF troop movement marked its first ever activation, at the request of one of its member states, for reasons of internal conflict.

But it was not just the activation that caught many people's attention. The Saudi force of 1,200 troops, combined with 800 troops from the United Arab Emirates (UAE), increased the total military and paramilitary strength in Bahrain by over 10 percent within several hours.[2] The additional troops sent a clear signal to the protesters that the GCC was prepared to act in order to keep the status quo within its area. In addition, the troop movement also raised questions as to how far the GCC was willing to go to have an internal military capability and what objective(s), besides maintaining the status quo, that capability was meant to serve.

The GCC was formed in 1981 originally as an economic union of like-minded and adjacent monarchies. Although never stated by the group itself, it is often said[3] by others that the GCC was formed in response to Iran's ascending Islamist threat after the overthrow of the Shah and the creation of the Iranian Islamic Republic in 1979. The GCC's charter speaks almost exclusively to economic issues but also discusses strengthening of ties and relationships between the six countries.[4] Although the GCC's

military security wing, the PSF, followed within five years of the original GCC charter,

its existence has never been codified within the charter itself or subsequent amendments.[5]

Since its inception, the PSF has been involved in few truly "joint" exercises with all six

countries' participation and has failed, as of yet, to achieve any military success

whatsoever. It has the distinction though of having each country's security and military

forces trained by U.S. military trainers and advisers on an individual country basis.

Unfortunately, this has not translated into a force structure that was cohesive enough to

field forces during Operation Desert Storm. In the run-up to the U.S. and Coalition

invasion of Iraq in 2003, the PSF also failed to participate in the Coalition effort as the

GCC member states disagreed on whether to support action against Iraq. Some GCC

countries did, in fact, offer substantial support in materiel and monies but the group did

not coalesce enough to succeed in doing so as a whole.

Triggers or events that would elicit mobilization of PSF have never been publicly

defined in GCC policy so its use, in the midst of the Arab Spring in March 2011, came

about as a surprise to inhabitants of the country as well as the surrounding region.

Bahrain's Foreign Minister, Sheikh Khaled Ben Ahmed Al Khalifa, stated several weeks

after the arrival of the PSF troops into Bahrain that the PSF would remain for some time

until "a threat to Gulf Arab countries from nearby Shiite power Iran was over."[6] This

statement seemed to indicate that, for the first time in the GCC's 30 year history, the

organization would keep an enduring military force of mixed troops and capabilities in

one area. The immediate concern that one would expect to arise from this call-up was

whether or not the GCC, with its limited experience in handling multi-national military operations, would have issues with synchronization, sustainment, and command and control of the troops. Tagging on to this concern was the fact that the GCC countries did not have an open declaration of PSF rules of engagement and the local population did not know what to expect from their neighbors' 'invading' forces.

The Invitation to Join

The GCC decided sometime shortly after its foray into Bahrain to include other countries with greater military expertise and numbers to its security operation. In May 2011, the GCC formally invited the Hashemite Kingdom of Jordan to join them as well as the Kingdom of Morocco, changing the organization from one based on geographic neighbors and economic partners to one in which the monarchial governments and their capacity to provide security strength came to the fore. This decision should also be considered in the light of the continued denial of Yemen's longstanding request to join. Yemen, a true 'Gulf' neighbor, made their request soon after the end of its civil war in the 1990s but has succeeded in being given 'observer status' only.[7]

There was an expectation that the two new member candidates (since actual membership mechanisms could take months, if not years, to complete)[8] would demonstrate their willingness to join by assisting in the security operation in Bahrain. There was an unconfirmed report that a Jordanian force of over 1,000 police officers traveled to Manama to assist with quelling the protests within days of the GCC membership invitation. Several Jordanian police officers were injured during particularly violent demonstrations soon after[9] and their presence in Bahrain became well known, although denied by the Government of Jordan. Morocco seems to have taken another path as there is no clear evidence that any Moroccan (aka Maghrebi) troops have been sent to

3

Bahrain. There has been acknowledgement from the Government of Morocco of the invitation but public reaction has been relatively subdued.

This thesis' primary focus, though, is the reasoning behind the GCC's sudden expansion, especially in light of the fact that the organization was founded on economic ties and geographical co-location. Looking at several possible motives, one must consider if the timing was associated with the panic raised by the Arab Spring and the threat of dissent and instability that came along with it. In tandem with that concern was the contention amongst some GCC leaders that the uprisings in several countries were not grassroots movements but were considered to be the work and influence of Iran and regional Shiite leaders.

The GCC is a unique set of countries that counts only monarchies as its members and only those led by Sunni Muslim kings, emirs, and sultans. In contrast, their populations are a mix of Sunni and Shi'a for the most part, although Bahrain is the exception. In the case of Bahrain the overwhelming majority of the population is Shi'a with strong ties to Iran as well as to the Shi'a of Saudi Arabia's Eastern Province. Should the inclusion of Jordan and Morocco be completed, this leadership profile would remain unchanged. Both Jordan and Morocco are also Sunni monarchies albeit considered more liberal, based on their respective constitutions and social freedoms within each country. Both leaders also enjoy popular support and have not been drastically affected by the calls for reform that their brethren kings have had thrown at them.

Historically, distrust exists on a governmental level between the Sunnis and Shi'as, dating back to their schism which occurred less than fifty years from the death of the Prophet Muhammad. This differs significantly from the schism which brought about

Protestantism, as the Islamic break occurred almost at the birth of the religion, not fifteen centuries later when there was already an established history and religious practice within Christianity. Differences and disputes between the two sects have kept their interpretations of the Quran, or Holy Book, distinct with few exceptions. When a country was ruled by a dictatorial leader or government, as in Saddam Hussein's Iraq and in Yemen before unification, religious differences between the sects were ignored or tabled as there were greater threats to the population. But the differences need to be considered as they have led to wars in times past, to include the Iran-Iraq war which from 1980 to 1988 pitted Iran's Shi'a Ayatollah Khomeini against Iraq's Sunni Saddam Hussein.

In considering if there would be a significant change to the GCC with the addition of Jordan and Morocco one can look at elements or instruments of national power, (to be defined shortly), and infer whether or not the GCC has something tangible to gain from enjoining the two Sunni monarchies into its club and if the same holds for the invitees.

The GCC and Invitees' Agendas

Jordan is buttressed between Israel and Iraq, and filled with millions of Palestinian and Iraqi refugees. GCC membership would transfer some of the larger countries' influence to Jordan–vital when speaking diplomatically and/or economically in a culture where 'wasta' or influence is considered more powerful than money or position.

Morocco is not under the same regional threat of the other seven countries but has the linkage of monarchy and the limitations that accompany it. With only democracies to its north in Europe, a tense relationship with Algeria to its east, and no membership in the African Union due to Morocco's stance on Western Sahara, it is politically and geographically isolated. The GCC membership may be more welcome when one considers Morocco's neighbors and their geo-political disagreements.

As a U.S. diplomat who has served at the U.S. embassies in Riyadh, Kuwait, Abu Dhabi, Manama, and at the Regional Embassy Office in Basrah, Iraq, and as a traveler who spent time living and working in Israel, Egypt, Turkey, and Tunisia I bring my own experience and understanding to this question as well. My discussions with locals of all backgrounds pointed to the commonality within their religion but when the topic turned to Sharia law and religious practice, there was a clear differentiation on how they viewed each other. From one point they all called themselves Muslim, followers of Islam, but on another—and this was much more from the Sunni view of the Shi'a rather than vice versa— the overwhelming opinion was that the Shi'a were 'mistaken' in their practices within the religion. This dispute within the Sunni/Shi'a religious community was spoken of only informally and, specifically, was never within official dialogue with foreign officials. For the purpose of this thesis the terms 'Sunni' and 'Shi'a' will be used interchangeably for both the singular and the plural of the person and the people.

Discussions will touch on Iran and its role in this development since the GCC was initially envisioned as a counter to Iran's growing strength and "largely as a response to Iranian activism in the Gulf after the 1979 Iranian revolution."[10] GCC's current growth may very well be correlated to developments within Iran's nuclear program and the increased threat that is perceived to come since the fall of Saddam Hussein in 2003. Iran's perceived political power has increased since the U.S. led invasion and subsequent failure of the development of a stable Iraqi government. Whereas before 2003 there existed a military balance to Iran's ambition in Iraq, today Iraq is seen as incapable of fielding any interference if Iran should strike any of the GCC countries. If anything, Iraq is now leaning much closer to its former nemesis and concerns about the possibility of political collusion between Baghdad and Tehran have been raised. This new Shi'a-to-Shi'a relationship is closely watched by the Sunni-led GCC.

The limitations of this study are based on time and geography. As the subject matter remains fluid and the invitations have not yet resulted in the full or partial inclusion of Jordan or Morocco into the GCC, all information and material for this thesis relates to incidents and developments that occurred on or before 31 January 2012. Although inferences may be made that the invitations were due in part because of the Arab Spring which affected North Africa, the Arab Gulf, and the Levant, this study is focused specifically on the GCC's six standing countries as well as Jordan and Morocco; it will not include other Arab countries except in passing. As the Arab Spring has now moved past its one-year anniversary of its inception, developments continue to unfold and play out, to include within the GCC, but it remains unclear what the final outcome will be or which leaders will remain in power when the dust finally settles.

U.S. Interest in the Region

On 5 January 2012, the Department of Defense released a short paper entitled "Sustaining U.S. Global Leadership: Priorities for 21st Century Defense"[11] which "is intended as a blueprint for the Joint Force of 2020."[12] Within the eight pages of text the GCC is named as an organization whose countries can assist the U.S. with its strategic objectives in securing regional peace and deterring Iran's nuclear ambitions. As such, any change within an organization of such strategic importance for the U.S. merits a closer look. The GCC's mention is significant as the U.S. relied heavily on the GCC countries for support in the build-up to Operation Enduring Freedom as well as for Operation Iraqi Freedom and continues to rely on them for both direct and indirect military support. The U.S.' ability to base troops, utilize transport within and without the region, as well as supply and sustain forces in the region remains the cornerstone of the U.S.' ability to project power in the region. The GCC remains wary and vigilant of its stronger neighbor to the East but has also increased purchases in military equipment in the past decade to further its own defensive capability[13].

For the U.S., the change within the GCC can equate to a strategic shift in how the GCC envisions itself economically and militarily and how it therefore views its place within the world order. Additionally, since the onset of Operation Enduring Freedom and Operations Iraqi Freedom there has been a distinct ebb and flow in the region's enthusiasm in hosting U.S. forces. Some GCC countries have reduced or removed U.S. troops' footprint (notably Saudi Arabia) while others allowed a thousand-fold increase in the period prior to the Iraq invasion and for the eight years that followed.

With the definitive end to U.S. military operations in Iraq in December 2011 and a firm commitment to end U.S. military operations in Afghanistan by 2014 the GCC faces a future where the question is no longer when will the Americans leave but who will support them once/if a drawdown occurs across the region. Even with the removal of troops from Iraq, there are U.S. Army troops and Air Force assets left in Kuwait, the Navy's Fifth Fleet in Bahrain, and further Air Force bases in both Qatar and UAE.

The Angle of Focus

Using the R-DIME (Religious, Diplomatic, Information, Military, and Economic) instruments of national power as best defined in the Department of the Army Field

Manual 3-05,[14] this thesis examines the advantages and disadvantages to each country in the following chapters as well as the impact, if any, on U.S. strategic engagements in the region. A point of note on the religious aspect of the study is that since all of the countries are Islamic, their religion, governance, and laws are all intertwined. This makes the religious aspect critical to their leadership as well as the rule of law.

Lastly, the GCC has a significant economic impact in the region but if their focus shifts to a military one, it may impact the U.S.' ability to maintain its own freedom of action within the GCC area of responsibility. As the GCC is closely tied to the political and economic objectives of each member country, any shift within its objectives may cause a corresponding shift in the framework of U.S. military movement. The U.S. currently has military bases in five of the six GCC countries and a Status of Forces Agreement with each of the six. The U.S. military may need to consider engaging the expanded GCC in a different way since the addition of Morocco is out of CENTCOM's Area of Responsibility and squarely in AFRICOM's portfolio. This is one pertinent reason that the Department of State always placed the Arab countries, even those of North Africa, together within one geographic bureau.

Primary Research Question

Based on the R-DIME assessments, what is the impact to the United States of the addition of Jordan and Morocco into the GCC?

Secondary Research Question

Based on the R-DIME assessments, what is the impact to the GCC of the addition of Jordan and Morocco into the GCC?

9

This thesis presents a review on what has been written on the subject and what is generally known of the countries under discussion in the next chapter while the methodology of finding answers follows in the third chapter. Within the fourth chapter is the analysis of information that addresses the research question and supporting information, while the conclusions and summary are contained in the fifth and final chapter, along with recommendations for future research.

---

[1]CNN Wire Staff, "Foreign Troops Enter Bahrain as Protests Continue," *CNN*, http://articles.cnn.com/2011-03-14/world/bahrain.protests_1_foreign -troops-bahraini-government-security-forc?_s=PM:WORLD (accessed 14 September 2011).

[2]James Hackett, ed., International Institute for Strategic Studies, *The Military Balance 2010* (London: Routledge, 2010), 246–247.

[3] GlobalSecurity.org, "Gulf Cooperation Council," http://www.globalsecurity.org/ military/world/gulf/gcc.htm (accessed 4 October 2011).

[4]Gulf Cooperation Council, "Gulf Cooperation Council Charter," http://www.gcc-sg.org/eng/indexfc7a.html?action=SecShow&ID=1 (accessed 10 September 2011), 2.

[5]Ibid.

[6]Fredrik Richter and Martina Fuchs, "Gulf Troops Staying until 'Iran' Threat Gone," *Jordan Times,* Reuters, http://www.jordantimes.com/?news=36659 (accessed 8 September 2011).

[7]Al Jazeera, "Arab Monarchs Respond to Spreading Revolutions," http://www. aljazeerah.info/News/2011/May/11 percent20n/Arab percent20Monarchs percent20 Respond percent20to percent20Spreading percent20Revolutions (accessed 26 September 2011).

[8]Arab News, "Morocco, Jordan Inch Closer to GCC," http://arabnews.com/ saudiarabia/article500539.ece?service=print (accessed 15 September 2011).

[9]Bahrain Freedom.org, "BahrainFreedom Blog," http://bahrainfreedom.org/ (accessed 31 October 2011).

[10]Andrew W. Terrill, *Kuwaiti National Security and the U.S.-Kuwaiti Strategic Relationship After Saddam* (Carlisle, PA: U.S.Army War College Strategic Studies Institute, 2007), 60.

[11]Department of Defense, *Sustaining U.S. Global Leadership: Priorities for 21st Century Defense* (Washington, DC: Government Printing Office, 5 January 2012), 2.

[12]Ibid., Introduction.

[13]Staff Writers, "Arabs Plan $63 Billion Air Power Buildup," United Press International, http://www.spacewar.com/reports/Arab_plan_63_billion_air_power_ buildup_999.html (accessed 4 October 2011).

[14]Department of the Army, Field Manual 3-05, *Army Special Operations Forces Unconventional Warfare* (Washington, DC: Government Printing Office, 30 September 2008), 2-1-2-10.

CHAPTER 2

REVIEW OF LITERATURE

This chapter is organized both by instrument of national power and by country. For Religion and Governance, which is inherently intertwined in Islamic countries due to dogma wherein the form of governance is regulated by religious belief, the information is provided on a country-by-country basis with some background included in order to provide relative historic context. For Diplomacy, Information, Military, and Economic sub-chapters the information is compiled by the subject itself and not by country. This approach is meant to serve as the clearest means to present the information and not intended to place one element above any other. Each is considered integral within this thesis and its place sequentially does not correspond to anything other than the arrangement of the acronym.

The GCC is often written about as an economic entity and, as such, much of the literature on its existence focuses on its economic capacity and capability. The GCC's own charter, signed in 1981 by the heads of state of each of the six member countries and revised in 2001, "laid down the ground(work) for the economic relationship"[1] but made no mention of other areas of common interest such as common defense or diplomatic influence. There is limited study of the GCC's capability militarily with the PSF. In 2000, a Naval War College paper raised the question of what was needed to enable the PSF to be a capable defensive force for the region.[2] There is, though, assorted depth of literature on other aspects of the countries as individuals and it is this literature that will be reviewed and consolidated in order to extract the common threads and themes as well as highlight those parts that are unusual or atypical for the countries in question. The review will encompass the six GCC member countries and the two invitees. Where there is discussion that pertains to all eight, the eight shall be referred but where it only refers to the six, the GCC will be mentioned as the unit of discussion.

Using the R-DIME model as described in FM 3-05,[3] this thesis focuses on comparing each element of national power individually, based on measureable and identifiable factors to see if there is an impact, and if so how much, on the inclusion of the two invitees. The choice of using these instruments of national power is because they are seen as "shaping an international environment,"[4] a possible indicator of how the GCC will be able to act and react in the future to regional events. The inclusion of Religion is essential as it closely ties in to the system of governance, rule of law, and culture of each of the eight countries. One more item of note is the role of tribal affiliation. Although reference to Tribe is not made as an element of national power, it is a significant link that ties a number of the ruling families and influential people within the Arab world. For that reason, a short explanation of the role of tribes is necessary.

Within Arab culture, tribal affiliation is considered to be a stronger and more enduring tie than national affiliation as Arab tribes have histories and lineages that go back hundreds of years and over thousands of miles of intertribal relationships while the Arab countries they now occupy are often less than a century old. When an Arab is asked in what order he puts his loyalty, oftentimes his response is immediate family, tribe, religion, and only then country. Tribes are not segregated by religious sects but there can be a tendency for some tribes to be mainly Sunni or mainly Shi'a. Many of the Arab tribes pre-date the birth of Islam and are historically linked to the land which their ancestors inhabited for centuries.[5] There is intermarriage between tribes and a history of

13

marriage for the purpose of strengthening relations between different tribes and clans, a subset of the tribes.

Religion/Governance–By Country

Unlike other monotheistic religions, Islam is a way of governance and law within Muslim countries. The court system is normally based on Sharia law with Islamic fundamentals of right and wrong as the basis for the laws of the land.[6] Islamic jurisprudence is interchangeable in countries where the Constitution holds Islam to be the guiding religion as criminal codes in most Sunni countries have similar or the same punishments for crimes as ascribed by the Koran. There is a caveat in that some civil courts in some Islamic countries also use a Napoleonic code based legal system for cases involving businesses but the criminal code is based on Sharia law. Additionally, Islam specifies how the banking and commerce systems should be run, as certain Western norms, such as charging fixed rates of interest for loans and taxing outside of certain precepts, are contrary to Islamic beliefs.

The religion of each of the countries within this thesis is Islam. All of the countries have a constitution, whether by name or in intent by decree, and each constitution names each country as an Islamic state.[7] Seven of the eight countries claim adherence to one of the two main sects or branches of belief within Islam, the Sunni branch. Sunni and Shi'a, the other main sect, both follow the Koran or Holy Book but Sunni also follow the Sunna or traditions of the Prophet Muhammed. The schism between Sunni and Shi'a was caused by a disagreement over the line of succession after the death of the Prophet and the choice of the next caliph. Shi'a do not consider the first three caliphs after Muhammed to be legitimate and believe that Ali, Muhammed's son-in-law, was the rightful heir to the Prophet directly after his death. Ali was the fourth caliph after the death of Muhammed and Shi'a consider only descendants from his line to be able to become the true leaders of Islam.[8] Sunnis "make up approximately 80 percent of the Muslim population worldwide"[9] and some Sunni believe that Shi'a are not real Muslims. This point of note exists among the educated as well as less-educated Sunnis and explains some of the dichotomies within the religion. Also to consider is that Shi'a countries do not historically have monarchies. The closest that they have come is Shah Pahlavi's Iran, pre-1979, but it was destroyed by fundamentalist Shi'a who placed a religious leader, Ayatollah Khomeini, at the head of the new Islamic Republic.

As Religion also plays a key role in leadership and governance as well as Diplomacy, the review will also look at each country's system of government with source material from the governments themselves, starting with the most populous within the GCC and going to the least populous, followed by Jordan and Morocco. There are common threads that can be found within all eight.

Kingdom of Saudi Arabia

Saudi Arabia is a monarchy founded on the consolidation of tribes by the Al-Sauds in the early 1900s within the Najd, an area which covers a large swath of central Saudi Arabia. Tribes from the Najd hold familial and historic (treaty) ties to tribes in adjacent countries, to include Yemen, Iraq, and Jordan.

Saudi Arabia, with its current land mass, was established in 1932 under the reign of King Abdulaziz Ibn Saud. Ensuing monarchs have all been his progeny but the advanced age of the remaining sons requires that the next King or Crown Prince be chosen from the successive tier of male descendants. The ruling family, encompassing

15

over 5,000 prince and princesses carrying the Al-Saud name,[10] knows that a medical ailment with the current King, Abdullah (age 88), or Crown Prince, Nayef (age 79), can cause a national crisis. At one point in 2010, both the King and Crown Prince Sultan (d. October 2011) were receiving medical treatment and their illnesses caused widespread concern since there was no clear process to nominate the next King should both he and the Crown Prince die at the same time.

Most of the senior Saudi princes hold ministerial portfolios or have served as provincial governors or both. The younger princes, those in their 60s, are viewed as moving up the ranks dependent upon the strength of their respective roles. For example, the positions of Minister of Defense and Minister of Interior are positions often associated with high capacity within the Royal Family. The current King has no full brothers but ten half-brothers remain. They will have influence on the choice of the next King, just as Roman Catholic Cardinals have influence over the choice of the next Pope in Rome even if they themselves are out of the running.

The King's title as "Custodian of the Two Holy Mosques" places special significance on him as he is required to do all within his authority to assure the safety of all Muslim pilgrims when they visit Mecca and Medina, a requirement of all practicing Muslims at least once in their lives if they are able. Saudi Arabia follows the strictest of Sunni sub-sects, Wahhabism, and the country's laws and courts are all based on Sharia, or Islamic law, as interpreted by the Wahhabis. Saudi Arabia is the most closed of all of the GCC countries and does not allow for social integration of men and women nor does it permit women the right to drive. Saudi Arabia also does not issue tourist visas and requires sponsorship for business travel to the country for non-GCC citizens.[11] These control measures are in place for security and for religious reasons and have resulted in a country that is westernized in a particular and peculiar fashion; banks with separate entrances for men and women, McDonalds which physically separate male and female customers, and a ban on women at sporting events where men might be present.

United Arab Emirates

United Arab Emirates (UAE) is the federation of seven 'princedoms' or Sheikhdoms which came into being officially in 1971 after a prolonged period as a British Protectorate. The formalization of the country known as UAE was completed upon the signing of its Constitution. UAE has land borders with Saudi Arabia and Oman while holding maritime borders with Iran in the crucial area of the Straits of Hormuz.

UAE is led by Sheikh Khalifa bin Zayed Al Nahyan, the son of Sheihk Zayed bin Sultan Al Nahyan who is considered the founding father of the UAE. Sheikh Khalifa was the Crown Prince for over 30 years before becoming President upon his father's death in 2004. Sheikh Khalifa is from the emirate of Abu Dhabi, which is also the capital of the country and the second wealthiest emirate after Dubai. Each emirate is led by its own Sheikh or prince and had its own rules that are a subset to those outlined by the Constitution.[12] The Vice President and Prime Minister positions are held by Sheikh Mohammed bin Rashid Maktoum, the ruler of Dubai.

The government of the UAE is run partially by appointees and partially by elected officials. The government has undergone some reform in recent years and it has given greater authority to the Federation National Council as part of the Executive Branch of government. The Federation National Council has representatives from each of the emirates for a total of 40 positions. Half of these 40 are appointed while the other half are elected to their positions.[13] Eight of the elected positions are currently held by women; a percentage that is comparatively high when one considers representation within the other GCC countries. Power sharing within the emirates themselves is quite common amongst the tribes but the ministerial positions of higher prominence within the Cabinet are held by members of the Abu Dhabi and Dubai ruling families. Lesser Cabinet positions can be held by non-royals to include professionals, as well as women. There is a court system which has both Sharia and secular courts, dependent upon the type of case presented.

UAE has international influence due in large part to its historic philanthropic tradition of working with lesser developed countries to improve living conditions. According to the UAE government, the country "supported projects in more than 120 countries in 2010"[14] in Asia, Africa, and the Americas. This financial assistance has helped create a reputation for the UAE as a country of largesse and almost infinite wealth. It should be noted that the UAE has the smallest native population with less than 15 percent of its inhabitants being Emirati[15] and the remainder a mix of mostly Asian and other Middle Eastern. The Emirati population is majority Sunni and its Shi'a minority is known to have familial ties to Iran.

Sultanate of Oman

Oman is the southernmost of the GCC countries, bordering both Saudi Arabia and Yemen with hundreds of miles of shoreline facing the Gulf of Oman and Iran at the Straits of Hormuz. It is the one GCC country which has historically had the farthest territorial reach, to include control of Zanzibar Island off the coast of East Africa as well as a part of present day Pakistan. The Sultanate has long-standing ties to the British and the British have fought for Oman's sovereignty against Saudi military forays into its territory in the 1950s.[16] Unlike the rest of the GCC and the two invitees, Oman is not Sunni Islamic but rather Ibadhi Islamic which has elements of both Sunni and Shi'a within it and "is known for its moderate conservatism."[17]

Oman is ruled by Sultan Qaboos bin Said who deposed his father in 1970 and brought Oman into the modern world. Sultan Qaboos is a direct descendant of Sultan Said bin Sultan, from whom all Omani Sultans since 1856 originate. The Sultan trained in Sandhurst and held an officer's position within the British military before returning to Oman and replacing his father. The Sultan is not married and has no known issue but there is a unique solution to the question of who will succeed the Sultan. According to Omani lore, Sultan Qaboos has already made a written recommendation that will be reviewed upon his death. If agreed to by the Sultan's closest advisors, the recommended successor will take the throne without dispute. In truth, the next Sultan must be chosen "by communal consensus and consent,"[18] a unique arrangement within the eight countries.

Oman's Executive branch is made up of the Sultan himself who holds the positions of Minister of Defense, Minister of Finance, Minister of Foreign Affairs, and Prime Minister, and an appointed Council of Ministers. The Legislative branch consists of two houses; the Majlis Al Shura (Consultative Council), an elected council which serves as a conduit between the people and the Council of Ministries and the Majlis Al Dowla (State Council) whose members are appointed by the Sultan. The third branch, the Judiciary, is divided up into local courts under the smaller states or provinces and the Supreme Court. Suffrage is universal for all Omanis over the age of 21 who are not serving in the military or security forces.

Oman's place within the GCC is unusual in that it keeps its foreign policy somewhat independent of its neighbors and has kept communications open with countries that others have shunned outright. An example of this was when Oman refused to break ties with Egypt over the Camp David Accords in 1978 even though the vast majority of Arab countries did so either literally or symbolically.[19] More recently, in 2011 Oman facilitated the release of the three American hikers who were arrested and charged with espionage in Iran. The Sultan's quiet diplomacy, especially with Iran, has provided Oman with a reputation for pragmatic and level-headed thinking even in the face of regional disapproval at times.

State of Kuwait

Kuwait is a constitutional monarchy that has evolved from the ruling Al-Sabah tribe from the early 1700s. The Al-Sabah tribe has led Kuwait since Ottoman times and was tied to the Ottoman Empire administratively from the Ottoman province of Basra (southern Iraq) but never ruled by Iraq. The Al-Sabahs did not rule autonomously as there existed merchant and trading families that held economic power within the country as well.[20] Between the Al-Sabahs and the merchants was an unwritten alliance that only fell apart when the merchant class declined in power with the advent of the oil-based economies of the 20th century. In 1896, as the curtain began to fall on the Ottoman Empire, Mubarak Al- Sabah, also known as Mubarak the Great, took control of the country and signed a treaty with Britain which allowed Britain to provide security for the country as its protectorate.

The position of Emir (Ruler) in Kuwait is hereditary and may pass to a son, brother, or nephew of the current Emir. Mubarak the Great was succeeded by his two sons who alternated control of the position and then three of their grandsons. The last change of Emir occurred in 2006 when Jabir Al-Sabah passed away in January and his incapacitated cousin Saad attempted to step into the role of Emir. Saad was not well enough to recite the oath of office and, after two weeks of negotiation, was removed from the line of succession by Jaber's brother Sheikh Sabah Al-Ahmad Al-Sabah.[21] Sheikh Sabah previously served as Kuwait's Prime Minister for several years but had also served as Kuwait's Foreign Minister for over 40 years. This extended tenure allowed him to personally know all of major political actors within diplomacy worldwide.

Kuwait is currently considered the most open of the GCC monarchies with the National Assembly of Kuwait (aka Parliament) representing both the Sunni majority and Shi'a minority, and, as of 2006, women as well. Women were given the right to vote as well as run for local electoral office in 2005. Suffrage is universal for all Kuwaiti citizens, 21 and older, who are not members of the military forces. Political parties are illegal in Kuwait but political associations are not. There are numerous associations where like-minded individuals can be put forth as a bloc vote in local and national elections. Parliament is not immune to royal influence as the 40-member National Assembly is required to tally their votes with the 15-member Kuwaiti Cabinet, all appointed by the Emir. This influence has led to some political deadlocks in the past ten years which, in turn, has resulted in Parliament being dissolved by the Emir and new elections called. Recent calls for reform, led mainly by the Shi'a minority within the Assembly, have challenged the Emir's authority but have not resulted in widespread violence or massive crackdowns on political dissenters.

State of Qatar

The country of Qatar occupies a peninsula jutting out from the Arabian Peninsula towards the east, into the Arabian Gulf. Its origin as a monarchy lies with its rule by the Al-Thani family originally from Bahrain. Territorial disputes between the two ruling families, the Al Khalifas and the Al-Thanis were partially settled by the British in 1868[22] but only in 2001 was there a permanent solution, crafted by the International Court of Justice[23] over ownership of the islands that separated the large island of Bahrain and the peninsula area of Qatar. Nevertheless, the Al-Thanis consider 1878 to be the year that their rule was solidified and modern day Qatar began to take form.

Qatar is a constitutional monarchy led by the Emir, Sheikh Hamad bin Khalifa Al-Thani. The Emir deposed his father, Khalifa bin Hamad Al-Thani in a bloodless coup in 1995 and then survived a counter-coup in 1996. Sheikh Hamad, a 1971 graduate of Sandhurst and former Commander in Chief of Qatari forces, rapidly introduced democratic reforms that allowed for greater freedoms, among them freedom of the press, freedom of religion, and freedom of assembly. Women were given the right to vote and run for office in 1999 just in time for the first ever elections, held on International Women's Day 8 March. Women work in many of the government ministries and are a visible part of the Qatari workforce.

The new freedoms as well as legal processes were codified in the Qatari Constitution which was drafted in 2003 and passed by referendum in 2005. The constitution confirmed the hereditary rule of the Al-Thani family but also established a legislative branch, the Majlis Al Shura or Advisory Council, which is one-third appointed and two-thirds elected by popular vote. Elections have been held three times since 1999 and there has been little to no call for Arab Spring type reforms among Qataris.

The Emir has worked to establish Qatar as a leader in negotiations and, similar to the ruler of Oman, has worked behind the scenes to keep lines of communication open with countries that are considered nefarious or contentious. The Emir and members of his family have remained in contact with Syria's ruling family, the Al Assads, throughout the cycle of violence which began in March 2011 even though Qatar was the first Arab embassy to close in Damascus.[24] They also supported Libyan rebels well before the international community agreed upon a level of support. Qatar provided financial as well as military assistance and sent hundreds of Qatari military to Libya to train the rebels.[25]

Qatar works within the GCC but is also known to work for its own interest outside the traditional GCC portfolio of petroleum. Qatar has had minor disputes with Saudi Arabia and understands that its size requires it to 'box above its weight' if it does not wish to be subsumed by Saudi Arabia's national interests.

Kingdom of Bahrain

The constitutional monarchy of Bahrain was a British Protectorate from 1830 until 1967. The ruling family, the Al Khalifas, have controlled Bahrain since 1783. They are tied to the much larger Bani Utbah tribe which, in turn, is linked to many of the major tribes of Saudi Arabia, Qatar, and Kuwait. The kingdom, previously called an emirate, became fully independent on August 15, 1971 when it declared itself separate from the union of the eight other emirates[26] which it had joined in 1968.

The Al Khalifa family is Sunni but the majority of the island population is Shi'a and has familial ties to the Shi'a tribes of Saudi Arabia's Eastern Province as well as to

Iran. The Al Khalifa family settled in Bahrain in the 18th century after previously dwelling in Kuwait and then Qatar. The family is led by King Hamad bin Isa Al Khalifa, formerly titled as Emir until 2002, but also has the Ruling Family Council which decides issues of internal dispute amongst family members. Although Bahrain counts its royals in the hundreds, vice Saudi where the number is in the thousands, the ruling family also has an iron hold on all of the key posts within all of the government ministries. There is no power sharing amongst other family or tribes within the government. Rule is hereditary and the King's eldest son is the Crown Prince.

Bahrain transitioned to a constitutional monarchy in 2002 and held municipal as well as (bicameral) parliamentary elections in 2002, 2006, and 2012. Women hold the right to vote and to run for office but only one woman has won a seat within Parliament. The Shi'a majority has also participated in the elections and Bahrain, before the Arab Spring began, had a vocal and visible opposition. Since March 2011, when the demonstrations in the capital Manama turned violent, the opposition has consolidated and has been joined by a number of Sunni Bahrainis who took exception to the attacks on largely peaceful protesters.[27]

As Bahrain is the smallest of the GCC states, the attention paid to its demonstrations and the government's response may seem off-balance but Bahrain has been previously subjected to overthrow attempts by Iranian elements. GCC members are and were concerned that the protests were not a grass roots movement but a bid by Tehran to turn the island into another Shi'a Islamic Republic. The two attempts to overthrow the ruling family, in 1981and in 1994, were investigated, documented, and considered to be the work of the Iranian regime.[28] No small wonder that the GCC did not

24

delay acting in concert with its smallest member in trying to suppress demonstrations that they considered to be originating from outside the kingdom.

Bahrain has endured the most violent of the Arab Spring protests within the GCC yet its ruling family shows no signs of weakening. King Hamad formed the Bahraini Independent Commission of Inquiry (BICI) to investigate possible human rights abuses during the protests. After five months of inquiry, the BICI returned a report stating abuses did occur and not simply within the Bahraini security forces but with the Jordanian security forces which were present. Further action against the abusers has not been taken.

Hashemite Kingdom of Jordan

Jordan is also a constitutional monarchy led by King Abdullah (al Hashemi). Jordan evolved from the British mandate of TransJordan after WWI and its current territory was formalized in 1946 bordering Israel, Iraq, Syria, and Saudi Arabia. The Hashemites, from whom the current King descends, have ruled in the region as a family and a tribe since the time of the Prophet Abraham in the 5th century and ruled the Islamic holy city of Mecca for seven hundred years before turning it over to the Al Sauds in 1925.[29] King Abdullah took the throne after the death of his father, King Hussein, in 1999 after ruling for 47 years. This long tenure as well as the ties that the Hashemites established over centuries of rule in the region means that Jordan's ruling family is tied to numerous tribes in the Najd as well as the Hijaz (the area along the western coast of Saudi Arabia, adjacent to the Red Sea). The Hashemites have more regional influence than belies Jordan's current territory as their family's lineage can be traced to the Prophet Mohammad.

The King, educated at Sandhurst, was a commissioned officer and served in the British military for several years before returning to Jordan. Similar to King Abdullah of Saudi Arabia, King Abdullah of Jordan holds the title of the Custodian of Al Haram al Sharif, the third holiest mosque in Islam which encompasses both the dome of the Rock and Al Aqsa Mosque[30] in Jerusalem. The King's responsibilities with this title require him to upkeep and refurbish the structures which, in turn, require him to work diplomatically and closely with the Israelis who control access to the sites. It is in this endeavor that Jordan has had to maintain dialogue with Israel, above and beyond any of the GCC countries or Morocco.

The King is also the head of the Executive branch which also includes the Prime Minister and the Council of Ministers. The Legislative branch has a bicameral Parliament with an appointed Senate and an elected Lower House. Unlike the GCC countries, political parties are legal in Jordan. The Judiciary comprises civil, religious, and special courts. Jordan is majority Sunni but has vast numbers of Palestinian refugees from the time of Israel's inception and subsequent wars, as well as Iraqi refugees fleeing sectarian strife, and now Syrian refugees from their government's crackdown. The refugees are a drain on Jordan's economy and infrastructure and pose special concerns for its internal security. Protests during Jordan's own Arab Spring led to the promise of reforms and some immediate changes within the government in 2011[31] but it remains to be seen if these reforms will satisfy Jordanians in the long term.

Kingdom of Morocco

Morocco is a constitutional monarchy which found its independence in 1956 after years of struggle against French rule. The government consists of three branches with a historically powerful Executive branch. The Executive branch consists of the King and his Prime Minister only. There is no Council of Ministers or other stated advisors within this branch. The Legislative branch has a bicameral Parliament with an elected Chamber of Representatives (lower house) and an elected Chamber of Counselors (upper house).[32] Similar to Jordan and in stark contrast to its brother GCC monarchies, political parties are legal in Morocco and participate in the elections for Parliament. Morocco's Judiciary consists of lower courts based on French civil law as well as Sharia law, and a Supreme Court.

Morocco is led by King Mohammed VI who began his reign in 1999 after the death of his father. The King's authority, despite the presence of political parties and elected officials, is considered absolute but the King has introduced governmental reforms since his reign began. In 2011, in light of the uprising in nearby Tunisia, the King set up a commission to draft a new Constitution which was then passed by popular referendum in July 2011.[33] Morocco, with a World Bank estimate of 32 million people, is by far the most populous of the eight countries but also contains the least educated and youngest population.

Morocco's location, far from the Arabian Gulf region but directly across from Spain at the Straits of Gibraltar, offers a European link to its people. Moroccans can be found working throughout Europe but especially in France where they have emigrated in large numbers since the 1960s, looking for work and a better life. Morocco's culture is the most nomadic when compared to the GCC countries where the citizens have little reason to abandon their government-assisted high living standard. This sets Morocco apart as its culture encourages the emigration of its people in order to improve their lives and the lives of their families through remittances back home.

Universal suffrage exists for all Moroccans at 18 years of age. Many Moroccans speak French as a second language rather than English, in addition to Arabic. Moroccan Arabic is considered to be very dissimilar to the formal Arabic spoken in the Gulf region and its pronunciation and grammar are difficult to comprehend for many Gulf Arabs. Morocco is over 98 percent Muslim and majority Sunni but there also exist Jewish, Christian, and Baha'i followers within the country.

The common thread for the eight countries within their governments is the presence of an absolute or almost-absolute monarch who rules within a hereditary system that is based on the rule of tribes from centuries ago within the deserts of the Najd as well as the deserts of Northwestern Africa. The monarchs keep the important government positions within their immediate family and share the lesser ones without. Religion also ties them together but none of the monarchs lay claim to the religious authority within their country, relying instead upon the leaders of the largest mosques to keep the faithful in line but also to maintain a non-confrontational approach with their rulers. The Ministries of Religion or Islamic Affairs within most of the eight countries pay a stipend to the imams, or religious leaders, within their mosques in a manner which allows them to focus on their profession but also keeps them somewhat beholden to their respective ministries.

Diplomacy

The GCC countries are closely connected diplomatically as their GCC mandate lays out the relationship between the six. Jordan and Morocco have full diplomatic relations with the GCC countries as individual countries but have also received GCC officers as representatives from the organization. Jordan and Morocco though also have the added strong diplomatic ties to Israel and France, respectively. These diplomatic ties may create possible future investment opportunities for the GCC countries that have limited to no business foothold within either country.

All of the eight countries are members of the United Nations (UN) as well as the League of Arab States, better known as the Arab League. Each has had a participating role in territorial or military disputes of one kind or another in the past 50 years (Jordan/Israel, Morocco/Algeria, Saudi Arabia/Qatar, Kuwait/Iraq, Bahrain/Qatar, Oman/Saudi Arabia, UAE/Iran) and all have demonstrated respect for the role of international diplomacy, mediation, and international treaties through their membership and participation in International Governmental Organizations.

The GCC currently has the capacity to use its group strength to bloc vote on referendums of interest to it. During the recent UN call for a Syrian ceasefire it was interesting to note that the GCC did not vote to castigate the Syrian regime but pushed for more soft diplomacy in terms of dialogue and possible mediation. The reasoning behind this is likely that the GCC understands that what may follow the regime might be worse than the regime itself. Should it choose to take a bloc stance, with its combined wealth and influence, it could garner support and perhaps sway a close vote but as a group of six it has not yet shown itself to publicly call for action. The addition of the two invitees could change that slightly but a look at their UN voting record will be an indicator of whether or not they are all already voting the same anyway.

Within the GCC charter there is an allowance for freedom of movement between the GCC countries. Should the two invitees be allowed full membership, this diplomatic benefit would offer their citizenry the prospect of legal employment on a larger scale. Many Jordanians already work within the GCC but are limited to one country or another for visa sponsorship. Diplomatic allowances that permitted a GCC visa would loosen the requirements for travel to the GCC in order to find work. This would address one of the GCC's main concerns as listed in its long-term development strategy, namely that "the imbalance in populations structure"[34] has resulted in too many foreign workers. Although Jordanians and Moroccans are technically foreign to the Gulf area, they are considered to be more homogeneous due to their tribal origins as compared to Muslims from Pakistan, the Philippines, and Indonesia.

Information

The eight monarchies are able to censor information that is broadcast within their countries to a point. Print media, radio, and television are all monitored with state-sponsored broadcasts being ubiquitous throughout the GCC region. There is also a presence by foreign media to include SKY from Hong Kong and BBC from the UK but the most influential media comes from within the region itself.

The news network, Al-Jazeera, began broadcasting from Qatar in 1996 and quickly developed a reputation for timely or on-the-spot coverage as well as allowing views which contradicted many of the political and religious views of the regional leaders to be aired. This was a novelty in a region where almost every piece of televised news was vetted for content before airing. Its programming originally seemed to hinge on anti-

American and anti-Israeli news pieces but by 2006 it evolved into a more balanced news channel with international impact.

In January 2011 Al Jazeera, broadcasting on TV and the internet, was one of the first to report on Cairo's anti-government protests and President Mubarak's response. Al Jazeera played video footage of the violence inflicted against ordinary Cairo residents and blogged hour-by-hour on developments as they took place in Tahrir Square in Cairo. Before having their offices ransacked and their news reporters thrown out of country,[35] Al Jazeera was able to show both sides of the protests and offered greater depth of coverage than any of the western news agencies who had limited-to-no Arabic speakers on site in the midst of the protests. Al Jazeera's coverage ended up, indirectly, supporting the call for change in Egypt. Its impact during the birth of the Arab Spring has yet to be fully realized.

Al Jazeera was originally funded by the government of Qatar for its first few years but now relies on private investors for its capital. Its reputation has vastly improved from its early years and it has won awards for its non-censorship of news pieces as well as content. Al Jazeera has also written several pieces on the inclusion of the two invitees into the GCC and its writers have reasoned that the decision reflects a desire on the part of the GCC to move away from Western-only military support, amongst other things.[36] Al Jazeera is not alone in speaking to the subject as Al Arabiya, a Saudi-supported regional television station, as well as numerous others weighed in within days of the invitations to surmise the reasoning behind them. Almost all mentioned either Iran or the Arab Spring uprising or both.

In Saudi Arabia the Ministry of Information office censors internet pages for unsuitable content, whether that content be politically, morally, ethically, or religiously incorrect. The office, affiliated with the Promotion of Virtue and the Prevention of Vice (aka Religious Police or Mutawwa'een), has been censoring what Saudis hear and see on the internet since the internet became popular in the late 1990s. The Saudi government does allow programming from around the region, to include Lebanon, Egypt, and the Gulf but restricts programs from Europe and the U.S. News print media is also heavily censored and even advertisements are vetted for visual content before being published.[37]

Kuwait, Oman, UAE, Jordan, and Morocco all have relatively open media but are sensitive to articles that portray their leaders or their neighbors' leaders in a negative light. This is not to say that criticism does not exist but it exists on a limited basis and is usually tied to specific government programs rather than their right to rule.

<u>Military</u>

The focus within the study of the military aspect of national power shall be the land forces component. As was pointed out to me by a GCC ILE student by chance, the PSF agreement is for the use of land forces only and does not include the request for either air power or naval power. As such *Jane's World Armies*[38] offers an in-depth view of each countries military inventory as well as its manpower to include security/paramilitary forces that are often more highly trained than the army within country.

Several issues immediately surface when one reviews the inventories as well as the summaries of the capabilities of the eight countries. First is that even though Saudi Arabia has the largest population within the GCC, with almost 27.5 million inhabitants, it has an army that is dwarfed by Jordan and Morocco, with just over 6 million and almost 32 million inhabitants respectively. It is undermanned and inadequate for the threat it might face from Iran. Saudi Arabia's defense relies upon the support of its allies, the U.S. and secondarily the UK.

Second is the fact that the UAE has spend the most, per capita, on air defense than any of the other eight countries, in part perhaps on their concerns over Iran and their shared maritime interests within the Gulf as well as their economic underpinning with international companies and investments. The UAE relies on its reputation as a safe place to invest and to visit as tourism is its other significant industry. The UAE's military purchasing program only slowed during the recent economic crisis and shows a concerted focus on air power.[39]

All of the GCC countries as well as Jordan focus on defensive capabilities and train to such. In addition, the smaller countries within the GCC, Bahrain, Qatar, Kuwait, and Oman, have extremely limited ability to hold their own against an attack for more than 24 to 48 hours.[40] Assistance will be necessary for any of the countries upon any offensive strike against them. All of their doctrines have had two main influences: British and American with British having heavy influence due to the early training experiences of several Gulf leaders as cited previously.

Serious issues within the GCC inventories of military equipment, in large part due to poor advice from defense and military contractors[41] as well as the countries who campaigned for specific weapons systems. Gulf countries have been sold weapon systems that have been at times flashy,[42] but mostly unable to deliver a comprehensive defense package for its clients. This is due to a certain extent on the piecemeal way the Gulf countries went about purchasing equipment. In a quasi-diplomatic method of purchasing, the GCC countries spread their wealth and buying power among companies from the five permanent UN Security Council members; China, France, Russian Federation, the U.S., and the UK. This has led to a disjointed inventory of tanks, guns, and anti-tank weaponry that has inconsistent standards of maintenance and training coupled to it. In Anthony Cordesman's 2005 book, *National Security in Saudi Arabia*, he speaks of the GCC's Peninsula Shield Force as a "hollow shell" due in large part to its inability to have a C4ISR, Command, Control, Communications, Computers, Intelligence, Surveillance and Reconnaissance package that would integrate the various military systems of each country, let alone the GCC as a whole.[43]

In comparison, Jordan does have C4ISR capability and has the modern facilities in country that permit and promote joint training for Jordanians, GCC member states, the U.S., and the UK. In contrast to Saudi's Army, Jordan's military also regularly participates in UN peacekeeping operations around the globe and allows women into non-combat roles within their conscription/volunteer force mix. Jordan's Army, Navy, and Air Force are joined by a Security component that includes a Special Operations Command (SOCOM) that trains with and next to the military elements. According to Jane's Sentinel Country Risk Assessments[44] the bulk of the Jordanian materiel comes from UK and the U.S. with some older Eastern Bloc weaponry as well. Jordan's military and security forces are considered to be the best trained of all the eight countries.

Morocco's Army is the largest of all of the eight countries with over 180,000 troops. The troops are bisected in two regions; the Northern Zone facing the threat of the Algerian forces across the border, and the Southern Zone securing the area known as

Western Sahara, a former Spanish colony that both Morocco and Algeria have claims on. The issue of Western Sahara is so contestable that Morocco was not permitted to join the African Union and is the sole country outside of it within the continent.[45] The Army is all voluntary with a minimum age of 20 to join. The Royal Moroccan Army, as it is known, has training teams on "loan to Equatorial Guinea and the UAE" and may have troops on contract with the Royal Saudi Army.[46] It is considered a competent force but its mission set with the bulk of the troops locked down in desert watch duty makes its ability to provide assistance to its new friends questionable to unlikely. There are an estimated 160,000 troops in the Southern Zone[47] and there is limited capability to move them quickly to a central transport area for onward movement anywhere.

For each of these eight countries, their military capacity and capability do not equate to the numbers proffered by their inventories. The Arab fighting ability should be considered in a cultural context. In Ken Pollack's in-depth look at the subject, *Arabs at War, Military Effectiveness 1948-1991*,[48] he notes that culture played a significant role in the defeat of Arab forces, whether they were from Yemen, Egypt, Saudi Arabia, Syria, or Libya. Mr. Pollack focuses on the fact that Arab culture is very hierarchical and does not promote creative thinking. This has led to repeated and severe issues with unit cohesion, tactical leadership, morale, and training to cite four of Mr. Pollack's nine factors for battlefield failure. Arab culture values information and influence so highly that for the military decision makers, tactical decisions are often made too late to implement and information is not passed to those who need it most.

Additionally, the future military integration of these countries requires a brief look at the Doctrine, Organizations, Training, Materiel, Leadership and Education,

Personnel, and Facilities (DOTMLPF)[49] available for them as a coherent group. This joint integration doctrine is currently used within the U.S. military but its salient points on ways interlacing the manpower, equipment, facilities, while increasing and improving the training and capabilities of the troops are valid for most military forces worldwide. This doctrine, as well as the cultural issue, needs to be considered alongside each country's military inventory in order to consider whether or not the PSF could become effective in the future.

Economics

At first glance, the accession of Jordan and Morocco appear to be an economic anomaly as the GCC countries' relationship is embedded in the economic strength of each country. The GCC countries are all considered wealthy and their citizens are provided with the highest level of education and health care gratis both in country and abroad if not available in country. The labor force configuration of skilled and unskilled labor will also be drawn out as one of the central pieces of the GCC's economic plan is the allowance of GCC member country nationals to work in each other's countries without the need for a work visa or residence documents. As most of the GCC countries have Muslim and non-Muslim, non-Arab, third-country nationals working within them, a shift that would allow Jordanians and Moroccans to take those jobs would change the face of the Gulf, quite literally.

The GCC countries also provide interest-free loans to its citizens in order to ensure that they are able to marry and set up a house for their families. Neither Jordan nor Morocco can come close to providing the same type of social services for their citizens as the World Bank considers Jordan and Morocco to be middle class and lower middle class respectively. This is in contrast to the GCC where all of the countries are considered wealthy.

Again, culturally there is a difference between the GCC member states and the invitees. Both Jordan and Morocco have a much higher ration of citizen service sector workers than the GCC and when one considers service jobs such as janitors, maids, waiters, and the like, one will see Jordanians and Moroccans in those types of jobs. The same holds for the health sector in that the GCC hires doctors and nurses from Western countries to work in their hospitals and to take care of their citizens but Jordan and Morocco are both treated by their compatriots.

Lastly on economic elements is the fact that the GCC countries are known for their petroleum products. Several of them, specifically Saudi Arabia and Kuwait, have been hindered from establishing other sources of national income due to limited options but all GCC countries are looking to expand their available resources. A close look at Jordan and Morocco's resources is called for since they may hold an indication as to part of the GCC's interest in their union. That and the possibility that replacing non-Arab workers with Arab workers would assist the countries of the GCC by keeping remittances within the region where they are most likely to be spent, thereby increasing the economies of the eight.

To that point, it must be stated that all of the GCC countries heavily rely on third-country nationals to man their military, in small or large part. Given the preponderance of desert and the requirements for border duty and desert watch, being in the military is not considered a coveted job. Looking at the possibility of Moroccans and (more) Jordanians joining the GCC military through the legal framework of the GCC charter may also throw light on the invitations. Again, the economic gain for the employer and the employee needs to be considered.

Methodology of finding the answers to the thesis question follows in chapter 3 while the analysis of the information and data is found in chapter 4. The conclusions and summary, along with any recommendations for further research into this topic, are located in chapter 5, the final chapter.

---

[1]Gulf Cooperation Council, "The Economic Agreement," http://library.gcc-sg.org/english/books/econagree2004.htm (accessed 31 October 2011), 1.

[2]Glenn P. Kuffel, Jr., "The Gulf Cooperation Council's Peninsula Shield Force" (Naval War College, Newport, RI, 2000), 18.

[3]Department of the Army, Field Manual 3-05, 2-1-2-10.

[4]Department of the Army, Field Manual 3-0, *Operations* (Washington, DC: Government Printing Officer, 2011), 4-1.

[5]Government of Jordan, "The Hashemites–Early History," http://www. kingabdullah.jo/index.php/en_US/pages/view/id/157.html (accessed 27 March 2012).

[6]Imam Muhammad Shirazi, *The Islamic System of Government* (London: Fountain Books, 2002), 2.

[7]"Saudi Arabia–Constitution," March 1992, http://www.servate.unibe.ch/icl/ sa00000_.html (accessed 15 March 2012); "UAE–Constitution," December 2, 1971, http://www.uaecabinet.ae/English/UAEGovernment/Pages/constitution_1_1.aspx (accessed 25 March 2012); "Oman–Constitution," 6 November 1996, http://www.servat. unibe.ch/icl/mu00000_.html (accessed 25 March 2012); "Kuwait–Constitution," 11 November 1962, http://www.servat.unibe.ch/icl/ku00000_.html (accessed 25 March 2012); "Qatar–Constitution," July 2, 2002, http://www.qatarembassy.net/constitution. asp (accessed 19 March 2012); "Bahrain–Constitution," 14 February 2002, http://www. servat.unibe.ch/icl/ba00000_.html (accessed 16 April 2012); "Morocco–Constitution," 13 September 1996, http://www.al-bab.com/maroc/gov/con96.htm (accessed 16 April 2012); "Jordan–Constitution," amended 1 September 1984, http://www.kinghussein. gov.jo/const_ch1-9.html (accessed 16 April 2012).

[8]Lesley Hazleton, *After The Prophet: The Epic Story of the Shia Sunni Split in Islam* (New York, NY: Doubleday, 2009), 62.

[9]Patheos, "Religion Library:Sunni Islam," http://www.patheos.com/Library/Sunni-Islam.html (accessed 4 April 2012).

[10]Data Arabia, "Family Tree," http://www.datarabia.com/royals/home.do (accessed 5 April 2012).

[11]Department of State, "Saudi Arabia–Country Specific Requirements," http://travel.state.gov/travel/cis_pa_tw/cis/cis_1012.html#entry_requirements (accessed 5 December 2011).

[12]Government of United Arab Emirates (UAE), "Constitution of UAE," http://www.uaecabinet.ae/English/UAEGovernment/Pages/constitution_1_4.aspx (accessed 25 March 2012).

[13]Government of UAE, "UAE Federal National Council," http://www.uae-embassy.org/uae/government/federal-national-council (accessed 25 March 2012).

[14]Government of UAE "UAE Foreign Aid," http://ww.uae-embassy.org/uae/foreign-policy/foreign-aid (accessed 25 March 2012).

[15]Department of State, "Background Note: United Arab Emirates," Bureau of Near Eastern Affairs, http://www.state.gov/r/pa/ei/bgn/5444.htm (accessed 29 December 2011).

[16]Library of Congress, "Country Studies," http://lcweb2.loc.gov/cgi-bin/query/r?frd/cstdy:@field(DOCID+qa0070) (accessed 20 March 2012).

[17]Department of State, "Background Note: Oman," Bureau of Near Eastern Affairs, http://www.state.gov/r/pa/ei/bgn/35834.htm (accessed 12 January 2012).

[18]Ibid.

[19]Joseph A. Kechichian, "Oman: a Unique Foreign Policy," Rand Corporation, http://www.rand.org/pubs/research_briefs/RB2501/index1.html (accessed 25 March 2012).

[20]Yacoub Y. Al-Hijji, *Old Kuwait: Memories in Photographs* (Kuwait: Center for Research and Studies on Kuwait, 2004).

[21]Ms. Andrea Gastaldo, personal experience during the brief succession crisis in Kuwait, January 2006.

[22]Embassy of State of Al Qatar, "History," http://www.qatarembassy.net/history.asp (accessed 19 March 2012).

[23]International Court of Justice, "Qatar v. Bahrain," http://www.icj-cij.org/common/print.php?pr=234&pt=1&p1=6&p2=1 (accessed 20 March 2012).

[24]Hugh Eakin, "The Strange Power of Qatar," *New York Review*, 27 October 2011, 43.

[25]Ibid.

[26]Department of State, "Background Note: Bahrain," Bureau of Near Eastern Affairs, http://www.state.gov/r/pa/ei/bgn/26414.htm (accessed 19 January 2012).

[27]Souad Mekhennet, "Bahrain Women Take Pride in Vital Protest Role," *New York Times*, 21 December 2011, http://www.nytimes.com/2011/12/21/world/middleeast/bahrain-women-take-pride-in-vital-protest-role (accessed 16 March 2012), 3.

[28]Mitchell A. Belfer, "The Fourteenth Province: The Irano-Bahrain Conflict in Perspective," *Central European Journal of International and Security Studies* (2011), 5, 7.

[29]Government of Jordan, "The Hashemites," http://www.kingabdullah.jo/index.php/en_US/pages/view/id/220.html (accessed 27 March 2012).

[30]Ibid.

[31]Department of State, "Background Note: Jordan," Bureau of Near Eastern Affairs, http://www.state.gov/r/pa/ei/bgn/3464.htm (accessed 19 January 2012).

[32]Department of State, "Background Note: Morocco," Bureau of African Affairs, http://www.state.gov/r/pa/ei/bgn/5431.htm (accessed 2 December 2011).

[33]Central Intelligence Agency, "The World Factbook: Africa: Morocco," https://www.cia.gov/library/publications/the-world-factbook/geos/mo.html (accessed 5 December 2011).

[34]Gulf Cooperation Council, Economic Affairs, "The Revised Long-Term Development Strategy for the GCC States 2010-2025," Economic Commerce and Industry Department, 12.

[35]Mark Sweney, "Al-Jazeera Office Attacked in Egypt Protests," *The Guardian*, http://www.guardian.co.uk/media/2011/feb/04/al-jazeera-office-attack (accessed 2 April 2012).

[36]Shenaz Kermali, "The GCC is Expanding its Army, but for What?" Aljazeera.net, http://english.aljazeera.net/indepth/features/2011/06/20116262649845386.html (accessed 8 November 2011).

[37]Ms. Andrea Gastaldo, personal experience living under Saudi regulations while assigned to Riyadh from 1998 to 2000.

[38]Jane's Defense & Intelligence Analysis, "Jane's World Armies-KSA," 2 December 2011, http://jwar.janes.com/subscribe/jward/doc_view_print.jsp?K2DocKey=/content1/janesdata/bi... (accessed 4 February 2012); Jane's Defense & Intelligence Analysis, "Jane's World Armies-UAE," 7 November 2011, http://jwar.janes.com/subscribe/jwar/doc_view_print.jsp?K2DocKey=/content1/janesdata/bi (accessed 4 February 2012); Jane's Defense & Intelligence Analysis, "Jane's World Armies-Oman," 16 November 2011, http://jwar.janes.com/subscribe/jward/doc_view_print.jsp?K2DocKey=/content1/janesdata/bi... (accessed 4 February 2012); Jane's Defense & Intelligence Analysis, "Jane's World Armies-Kuwait," 3 January 2012, http://jwar.janes.com/subscribe/jward/doc_view_print.jsp?K2DocKey=/content1/janesdata/bi... (accessed 4 February 2012); Jane's Defense & Intelligence Analysis, "Jane's World Armies-Qatar," 16 September 2011, http://jwar.janes.com/subscribe/jward/doc_view_print.jsp?K2DocKey=/content1/janesdata/bi... (accessed 4 February 2012); Jane's Defense & Intelligence Analysis, "Jane's World Armies-Bahrain," 22 June 2011, http://jwar.janes.com/subscribe/jward/doc_view_print.jsp?K2DocKey=/content1/janesdata/bi... (accessed 4 February 2012); Jane's Defense & Intelligence Analysis, "Jane's World Armies-Morocco," 3 November 2011, http://jwar.janes.com/subscribe/jwar/doc_view_print.jsp?K2DocKey=/content1/janesdata/bi (accessed 4 February 2012); Jane's Defense & Intelligence Analysis, "Jane's World Armies-Jordan", 27 June 2011, http://jwar.janes.com/subscribe/jwar/doc_view_print.jsp?K2DocKey=content1/janesdata/bi (accessed 4 February 2012).

[39]Staff Writers, "Arabs Plan $63 Billion Air Power Buildup."

[40]Jane's Defense & Intelligence Analysis, "Jane's World Armies-Oman"; "Jane's World Armies-Kuwait"; "Jane's World Armies-Qatar"; "Jane's World Armies-Bahrain."

[41]Anthony H. Cordesman and Nawaf Obaid, *National Security in Saudi Arabia* (Washington, DC: Center for Strategic and International Studies, 2005), xxiv.

[42]Ibid, 137.

[43]Ibid, xxii.

[44]Jane's Defense & Intelligence Analysis, "Jane's Sentinel Country Risk Assessments–Jordan at a Glance," http://sentinel.janes.com/subscribe/sentinel/doc_view_print.jsp?K2DocKey=content1/jane (accessed 16 September 2011).

[45]Department of State, "Background Note: Morocco."

[46]Jane's Defense & Intelligence Analysis, "Jane's World Armies-Morocco," 3.

[47]Ibid., 2.

[48]Kenneth M. Pollack, *Arabs At War, Military Effectiveness, 1948-1991* (Lincoln, NE: University of Nebraska Press, 2002), 590.

[49]Department of the Army, Field Manual 1, *Army* (Washington, DC: Government Printing Office, 2005), 4-10-4-11.

CHAPTER 3

METHODOLOGY

This thesis will use a qualitative and quantitative approach to present and analyze the information that is under consideration. Taking Harry F. Wolcott's[1] approach to qualitative research that "all research is based on observational data"[2] and working with a quantitative method for economic indicators that will include World Bank data[3] and a compendium of International Monetary Fund, United Nations, and Central Intelligence Agency data already tabulated, the combination of the two types of research will provide indicators of the impact of the two invitees into the GCC. Note that the use of Central Intelligence data will only occur when there is no other reputable source data available and where the Central Intelligence data is considered a viable alternative for on-the-ground information through its reporting. Within the analysis, the timing of the invitation will be considered in order to predict if the civil unrest within the GCC and other Arab countries is linked to the invitation or whether or not there were other reasons of note to consider inviting them in and the timing was happenstance.

Religious, Diplomatic, and Information

For the Religious (Governance), Diplomatic, and Information portion a qualitative approach will allow a comparison by country law and norms of how, if the two invitees are enjoined into the GCC, that may impact each of those elements. Side-by-side comparisons of the eight Constitutions, of how each country sees itself and its economic and defense requirements will also highlight if there would be significant accommodations that would have to be made in order to allow Jordanian and Moroccan citizens to live, work, and soldier within the GCC. Within the leadership realm, a simple chart of the ages and length of reign of the current monarchs as well as the ages of the Crown Princes may demonstrate how much influence they have been able to have on their sovereign policies and, in turn, how long the GCC will be able to hold on to its current shared interests.

The voting tally within the UN would also be of use but the vast majority of General Assembly resolutions are passed without a recorded vote. Due to this the eight countries' voting record within the UN will not be considered in determining if the two invitees will be able to work diplomatically together. The individual GCC countries' vote within the Arab League on Morocco's occupation of Western Sahara could be considered since this is a subject that is contentious in international community. The eight countries' membership in the Arab League, with Jordan and Saudi Arabia being two of the seven founding members, will be considered with a review of any issues that have been controversial in the past several years.

Military

For the military assessment, there will be a quantitative as well as qualitative look at the land based army and security/paramilitary force inventories of each of the eight countries as well as their manpower. The inventories, in and of themselves, may show the ability to defend their respective countries and a graph of the national defense budget for each country will also indicate each country's investment on defense but a qualitative look at their manpower, not simply in numbers but in how well they are trained and if they have training experience outside their own country, will help establish the likelihood of the new invitees ability to support the PSF. Within the Middle East region, the internal security forces often have more training and weaponry as they are used kinetically more often than the military. Cases such as the takeover of the Grand Mosque in Mecca and numerous terrorist or security incidents in Saudi Arabia, Kuwait, Jordan, and Bahrain have required all of the Middle East area countries to keep a high level of police/paramilitary readiness. Those same forces would be utilized in case of external threat or attack and will be included in quantitative military tallies as such.

Jane's World Armies[4] offers thirty different variables within each country study. Due to the fact that not all of the countries have any information listing under each category and that some categories are not applicable for assessing integration of the militaries within this study, I will be considering seven of the thirty for weighted comparison: Adaptability, Readiness, Deployment/tasks/operations, Command and Control, Demographics, Morale, and Professionalism. The seven will be charted on a matrix with a weighted score for each variable. One category will be added to the seven which will cover the internal joint training between the military forces and security forces of each country.

Lastly, no look at military would be complete without considering each country's military doctrine, land forces as well as joint doctrine and combined arms doctrine and whether the individual country doctrines could fit into a larger group or if the GCC has a doctrine that could be extended to the invitees for the purpose of working within the PSF. This will be completed in narrative form with a link to the Command and Control aspect since doctrine ties closely into Command and Control within most Western nations' studies.

Economic

For the economic assessment of each country, graphing out each of the eight's population, unemployment, GDP per capita, and literacy levels will show how the two invitees stand in comparison to the GCC and how they may impact the GCC's ability to retain its standing as an economic bloc worth 1.4 trillion[5] in light of Jordan and Morocco's own economic health. Culling directly from the World Bank Data for each country as well as the International Monetary Fund's listing of real Gross Domestic Product (GDP)[6] will provide insight as to the fiscal differences between the eight. In addition, there will be a comparison of natural resources to see if the newcomers have the ability to add to the one-dimensional petroleum economies that most of the GCC adhere to. In light of their geographical locations and their diverse trading partners, there will be a comprehensive look at the increase in trade the two countries may be able to contribute as either direct traders or intermediaries to the U.S. as Jordan, Morocco, and Oman are the only countries within the eight that have a Free Trade Agreement with the U.S.[7]

If the invitee countries are allowed full employment within the GCC, their remittances back home are likely to change the economic outlook of their own countries. Currently the countries with the largest number of third country nationals in the GCC are Pakistan, India, Indonesia, and the Philippines. Remittance numbers from the Philippines are available[8] and can be used as an indicator for how much of an impact a change in employment migration would make for Jordan and Morocco. Remittances for the other countries are difficult to calculate and will not be considered within this work.

By considering how synchronized these eight countries could become (legally, politically, and ideologically), and reviewing their leadership, their governance framework, their military capacity, and framing their economic health with the factors listed above, the impact of the two invitees should be clear to infer for them as well as the GCC. As mentioned in chapter 1, the role of the U.S. within the Arabian Gulf remains vital to the U.S.' security objectives. The impact of the GCC's decision will also infer what this may mean for the U.S. and its extended presence within the Gulf region, if anything. No study could ignore the ramifications if the increase in GCC membership resulted in an increase in internal defense capabilities for the GCC and the possibility of fewer boots on the ground for the U.S. That is not to say that it will be a foregone conclusion but only that it is one possibility among many.

Chapter 4 follows with an analysis of the R-DIME elements one by one, with the Religious, Diplomatic, and Information starting off the chapter with a narrative comparison. Most Military and Economic factors will be graphed out as described before, within the context of variables previously mentioned, as well as narrated to work out the impact of factors. The chapter will end with a matrix of the R-DIME elements juxtaposed with the countries to summarize the findings for each. Chapter 5 will end the study with a summary and conclusions as well as any recommendations for further study.

---

[1]Harry F. Wolcott, *Writing Up Qualitative Research* (Los Angeles, CA: Sage Publication, 2009).

[2]Ibid., 79.

[3]The World Bank Group, "Countries and Economies," http://data.worldbank.org/ country (accessed 4 February 2012).

[4]Jane's Defense & Intelligence Analysis, "Jane's World Armies-KSA," 2 December 2011, http://jwar.janes.com/subscribe/jward/doc_view_print.jsp? K2DocKey=/content1/janesdata/bi... (accessed 4 February 2012); Jane's Defense & Intelligence Analysis, "Jane's World Armies-UAE," 7 November 2011, http://jwar.janes. com/subscribe/jwar/doc_view_print.jsp?K2DocKey=/content1/janesdata/bi (accessed 4 February 2012); Jane's Defense & Intelligence Analysis, "Jane's World Armies-Oman," 16 November 2011, http://jwar.janes.com/subscribe/jward/doc_view_print.jsp? K2DocKey=/content1/janesdata/bi... (accessed 4 February 2012); Jane's Defense & Intelligence Analysis, "Jane's World Armies-Kuwait," 3 January 2012, need url (accessed 4 February 2012); Jane's Defense & Intelligence Analysis, "Jane's World Armies-Qatar," 16 September 2011, http://jwar.janes.com/subscribe/jward/doc_view_ print.jsp?K2DocKey=/content1/janesdata/bi (accessed 4 February 2012); Jane's Defense & Intelligence Analysis, "Jane's World Armies-Bahrain," 22 June 2011, http://jwar.janes. com/subscribe/jward/doc_view_print.jsp?K2DocKey=/content1/janesdata/bi... (accessed 4 February 2012); Jane's Defense & Intelligence Analysis, "Jane's World Armies-Morocco," 3 November 2011, http://jwar.janes.com/subscribe/jwar/doc_view_print. jsp?K2DocKey=/content1/janesdata/bi (accessed 4 February 2012); Jane's Defense & Intelligence Analysis, "Jane's World Armies-Jordan," 27 June 2011, http://jwar.janes. com/subscribe/jwar/doc_view_print.jsp?K2DocKey=content1/janesdata/bi (accessed 4 February 2012).

[5]Dubai Media Incorporated, "GCC GDP to Accelerate to 6.8 Percent in 2011," http://www.emirates247.com/business/economy-finance/gcc-gdp-to-accelerate-to-6-8-in-2011-2011-06-03-1.400707 (accessed 26 September 2011).

[6]International Monetary Fund, "IMF Country Information Page," http://www.imf. org/external/country/index.htm (accessed 4 February 2012).

[7]Department of Commerce, "Free Trade Agreements," Office of the United States Trade Representative, http://www.ustr.gov/trade-agreements/free-trade-agreements (accessed 12 March 2012).

[8]Central Bank of the Philippines, "Overseas Filipinos' Remittances-Bangko Sentral ng Pilipinas."

CHAPTER 4

ANALYSIS

The purpose of this analysis is to ascertain the impact on the U.S. as well as the GCC of the addition of the Jordanian and Moroccan monarchies into the GCC. The impact is being considered from the angle of the traditional instruments of national power; Diplomacy, Information, Military, and Economic, with the addition of Religion and Governance. In order to best determine how these instruments can be measured, a combination of qualitative and quantitative information is compiled in both narrative and data format within this chapter. The chapter commences with Religion, followed by Diplomacy, Information, Military, and Economic. Some information may overlap within the instruments but information from each can be inferred independently. At the end of the chapter is a matrix that integrates the information from the R-DIME assessment to answer the primary research question of what is the impact to the U.S. of the addition of Jordan and Morocco into the GCC as well as the secondary question of the impact on the GCC itself once the two invitees become part of the group.

Religion/Governance

As stated in chapter 2, the religion of all eight countries is Islam. With the exception of Oman, the leadership under discussion adheres to the Sunni sect of Islam but with various degrees of interpretation. The most restrictive and narrow interpretation is under Saudi Arabia's Wahhabi school of Sunni Islam where the segregation of the sexes is required by law and non-Muslim houses of worship are not permitted to exist.[1] The most open interpretation may be regarded as under Moroccan rule, due to its close proximity to Europe and the influence of the African as well as European cultures. Morocco seems to permit a more open society, perhaps in part due to its vital tourism industry and the cultural infusion from its émigrés to France and Spain.

Oman is the religious outlier, following the Ibadhi school of Islam which is considered a mix of both Sunni and Shia traditions and practices. The Ibadhi school is relatively small in the Islamic world and Oman is the sole Islamic country with an Ibadhi majority. Even though it is distinct from both Sunni and Shia sects, there are no restrictions on Ibadhis interacting with them nor is there a restriction on Sunnis or Shias in the reverse.

From a sovereign standpoint, all eight countries mention Islam within the first few articles of their respective constitutions. For Saudi Arabia and Qatar, naming Islam as the country's religion is stated within the first article. For Bahrain, Kuwait, Oman, and Jordan, its importance is laid out in the second article. For Morocco it rates mention in the sixth article and for the UAE it is defined in the seventh article. What is more telling is that in each and every country's preamble or within the first few articles is the identifier of each country as an Arab state, within the greater Arab nation.[2] This Arab identifier could be viewed as something more significant than one country's specific religious following. It goes to the country's self-image as belonging to a greater Arab entity, one that is larger than the eight countries involved in this study but one that interlinks all eight together and keeps it separate from other Islamic nations such as Iran.

Delving further into the respective constitutions into the matter of jurisprudence, the authority for the laws of the land is laid out for six of the eight countries. Kuwait, Bahrain, and Saudi Arabia's constitutions include statements that their laws are "in accordance with Islam."[3] Qatar, Oman, and Jordan mention that Sharia law is "the main source of (its) legislation"[4] while also including other courts to include commercial case courts. In the unusual cases of Morocco and the UAE, there is no mention at all of Sharia or other basis for the laws of the land. For Morocco and the UAE, freedoms and government responsibilities are outlined but there is no indication as to the foundation that underpins their respective legal codes.[5] Although the framework for their legal systems is not spelled out, this does not imply that none exists but rather that their respective constitutions chose not to expound upon it.

Continuing on to the selection of ruler, each constitution weighs in clearly and absolutely. For each of these monarchies, the laws of succession and hereditary rule are spelled out in depth and permit little room for interpretation. None of the eight countries fails in its duty to spell out for the populace how their ruler is chosen and under what circumstances he may be replaced, if any. There is no allowance for a female sovereign and hereditary rule follows the male line of descendants only. Although clear on details for rule, there are no specified restrictions on requirements for marriage, so it is conceivable that there could be intermarriage amongst the eight ruling families themselves. Some constitutions also include provisos specifying the type of positions that the monarchs may hold within government but most are cut from the same cloth on how the issue of succession is regarded.

All eight base their monarchal governments on the trilateral model of executive, legislative, and judicial, albeit the executive (read monarch) is overwhelmingly stronger than the other two in most cases. At the very least, the executive is designed to heavily influence legislative and judicial decisions.[6] Most constitutions also include the

51

requirements for the establishment and authority of the Councils of Ministers, the Judiciary, and Representatives or Assemblymen within their respective domains. Again, within the context of governmental arrangement, all eight are comparable to one another.

Diplomacy

Each of the countries is a full member of the UN as well as the League of Arab States (aka Arab League). Although there is no public listing of the voting records of the UN, the eight as a group would be too small within the UN populace of 193 member states[7] to effect change without significant additional support from other nations or voting blocs. As an eight-member bloc within the 22 countries[8] of the Arab League though, the GCC plus two will have greater weight and influence, which can translate into consequential action at the UN level. The Arab League is looked to by the UN for guidance on possible resolutions within its area of authority. In March 2011 the Arab League pushed hard for action against Libyan leader Qaddafi, calling for a "no-fly zone" that would lessen his ability to attack rebel forces and innocent civilians on the ground.[9] The call by the Arab League was considered the catalyst for a UN Resolution and subsequent NATO action in Libya.[10] This was followed in November by the Arab League's suspension of Syria from its group of 22 in a move called "unusually robust"[11] for the group. This may be seen as a precursor to greater international diplomatic clout by the Arab League and the GCC within it.

At the time of the invitation, and currently, there are no overriding issues of contention within the GCC plus two. The situation with Morocco and Western Sahara concerns Algeria and the African Union but is not a topic of discussion within the GCC at the moment.[12] Each of the eight has full diplomatic relations with the others and all eight also have representative missions within each. As monarchs who all come from tribal backgrounds, the eight are all personally known to each other and territorial issues that were previous sources of raised tensions have been resolved.[13]

Diplomatically their differences lay with their relationships to Israel, more than any other country. Jordan has full diplomatic relations with Israel while Morocco and Oman both suspended their diplomatic relations with Israel after the outbreak of the second Palestinian 'intifada' (uprising)[14] in October 2000. Since diplomatic relations have been 'suspended' and not 'severed' there is the possibility that they can be restored and that the Moroccans and Omanis can each have a future role in shaping the regional peace process. Jordan's diplomatic ties with Israel are considered a geographical necessity. Interestingly enough, Jordan had greater diplomatic issues with the GCC in 1991 when it sided with Iraq after the invasion of Kuwait. This caused widespread anger amongst the GCC and it took the better part of the decade to fully restore the diplomatic relationships and trust with Jordan.

One key point to add is that all eight monarchs have a certain amount of influence based on their ages as well as the length of their thrones. Comparing their ages and their length of time as monarch also indicates how much impact they can have on their particular reign. That fact will have diplomatic impact as the new monarch, regardless of country, will either hold the status quo and keep relations with the rest of the GCC as they are or decide to alter them to some degree. As this may occur sooner in some countries than in others, it should be considered within the diplomatic aspect of the thesis.

Table 1.   Age and Current Length of Reigns for the GCC + 2 Monarchs

	KSA	UAE	OMAN	KUWAIT	QATAR	BAHRAIN	MOROCCO	JORDAN
Age	88	64	71	82	60	62	48	50
Years as Monarch	6 yrs. King + 8 yrs. Regent	7 yrs.	41 yrs.	6 yrs.	16 yrs.	13 yrs.	12 yrs.	13 yrs.

Source: Created by author. From information compiled from official government websites, April 2012.

Information

For each of the eight monarchies, there exists some form of press or media censorship in each country. In a Freedom House ranking of media freedom in 154 countries, Kuwait is listed as "partially free"[15] while the other seven are considered "not free" on press freedom. Censorship goes beyond print and radio into access to internet sites and 'real-time' media such as Twitter. This control has served the monarchies well and has been used as a security tool to check on websites that may incite opposition to the leadership. The fact that all eight have some sort of censorship places them all at the same table. The limits on freedom of media and expression are well publicized by the state sponsored media, and the parameters in which the media work themselves are relatively clear. Journalists from one end of the GCC spectrum such as Qatar know what to expect in Saudi Arabia or Morocco or elsewhere and often self-censor. Opposition to the monarchies is often found outside the countries but internal opposition is often muted and aimed at policies rather than people. This holds for the two invitees as much as for the GCC and should not be considered a deviation from their own practices.

Additionally, the information that is disseminated can be synchronized within the region if the joint leadership so chooses. The message that goes out to the region can be coordinated in part due to the state's control of media, whether in large part or in lesser. The GCC addresses the media as a tool of education, not of limitation, and is looking to create a "media-interlink between GCC states"[16] that can enhance and improve the development capacity of the entire region. The use of media as a training tool would mean that it could be used to influence the economic arena by assisting with training for the GCC residents and helping to increase the skilled pool of workers. This would contrast its current use as being more of a tool of constraint.

There is an information consideration that has to be made with respect to Morocco. The GCC's economic agreement includes a proviso for unhindered travel between the GCC countries. Although there will be an economic benefit to Morocco if it opens up to greater tourism from the Gulf nations, there is also the greater likelihood that there will be a clash of cultures. The same will occur if there is a significant increase in employment within the GCC for Moroccans. Even if the countries have the same or similar basis, the culture of a nation within Africa and closely affiliated with Europe does not have the same outlook as those who are more internally focused. The influence may be indirect but there can be little doubt that Morocco's heritage and its great number of other-than-Arabic speakers, to include indigenous languages, French, Spanish, and others, will have an impact on the cultural mores of the GCC.

Military

The Headquarters for the GCC's PSF is in Hafr Al Batin, Saudi Arabia. The site is approximately 65 miles from the border with Kuwait and the city itself is one of four

55

military cities, constructed with the express purpose of housing and training troops for service to the Kingdom. In the case of Hafr Al Batin, it was designed for a brigade plus of 6,000 men and "re-inaugurated" in 2003 by Prince Sultan Bin Abdul-Aziz, Saudi Minister of Defense.[17] The location of the GCC headquarters allows Saudi Arabia to have primary control but also allows for its growth as a training site since there is nothing to impede its expansion except desert in all directions. The GCC's original concept for the PSF was for two brigades worth of troops, for a total of 10,000 men.[18]

The make-up of the GCC military arsenal is, as mentioned in chapter 2, a collage of military equipment from the UN Permanent Security Council Member countries but Jordan and Morocco face different challenges with their inventory. Following in UAE's footsteps,[19] Jordan has begun to build its own "indigenous defence industry"[20] and is working to enhance its inventory by manufacturing its own upgrades. It currently is changing its (UK) Challenger 1 tanks to accommodate enhancements and has worked on its other Main Battle Tank (MBT), the (U.S.) M60.

Jordan's military is reputed to be the premier trainer of other militaries in the region and has trained GCC military staff in Jordan as well as in GCC countries. Jordan has focused much of its training on Special Operations and in 2009 opened the King Abdullah Special Operations Training Center (KASOTC) for Jordanian as well as other friendly-nation training. As a result, the GCC countries consistently look to Jordan when hiring military and security forces staff. Jordan's armed forces are considered "among the most professional in the region"[21] and are both well-trained and well-organized with a joint headquarters to help synchronize its organizations.

Morocco's continuous military presence on the southern border with Western Sahara has kept its military at a high state of readiness. Its military is considered well-trained but it faces greater challenges with integration into the GCC than Jordan, in part due to moving from a conscription army to an all-volunteer force in the past five years. In addition, Morocco has the oldest inventory; its MBTs are a collection of T-72s, M60A1s, M60A3s, and M48A5s, most of which came into service almost twenty years ago. Morocco keeps an estimated half of its armored vehicles in storage[22] in case the situation in Western Sahara returns to an active state of war.

Both Jordan and Morocco allow women to serve in segregated units within their armed forces as well as their security forces. This is a social and religious challenge for full military integration into the PSF, especially as the Headquarters and main training center is in the most conservative of the six countries, Saudi Arabia. The PSF is an organization that is based on the agreement to provide mutual defense but without clear parameters as to how that defense is proffered. It is a land-force integration focus which does not prohibit females per se but most of the original signatory countries still do not permit females to serve, with the exception of the UAE[23] although in what capacity is not clear. It may be possible to require that the female units not deploy on PSF operations, if and when the occasion arises where the two invitees are asked to assist under the parameters of a mutual defense agreement.

In looking closely at Jane's World Armies as well as Jane's Executive Summary for each of the countries the quantitative numbers that will be reviewed are the total number of military troops in each countries land forces as well as the number in the respective paramilitary/security forces as these are used in tandem when there is an internal threat to the country. In addition the military expenditures for each country based on a percentage of their respective GDPs[24] will be reviewed to compare the spending pattern of the two invitees and to see if this is in line with the GCC. This particular figure can be considered an indicator of how seriously each country considers its defense and an area where the wealthier GCC countries can assist in defense purchases for others through grants or loans. Since the GCC includes a mutual defense pact as well as an economic agreement, similar spending may indicate similar outlook on how high a priority defense is on each country's strategic outlook.

Source: Jane's Executive Summaries, "Jane's World Armies," 2011-2012, http://jwar.janes.com/subscribe/jwar/doc_view_print.jsp?K2DocKey=/content1/janesdata/bi (accessed 4 February 2012). Note that some data for security forces (i.e. police, border police, national guard) was not available for each country.

Table 3.   Military Expenditure as a Percentage of GDP and USD Amount (in Billions)

KSA	UAE	OMAN	KUWAIT	QATAR	BAHRAIN	MOROCCO	JORDAN
10%	3.1%	11.4%	5.3%	10%	4.5%	5%	8.6%
56.03	11.10	7.62	9.07	17.32	1.19	5.09	2.44

Source: Central Intelligence Agency, "Military Expenditures," 13 April 2012, https://www.cia.gov/library/publications/the-world-factbook/geos (accessed 16 April 2012); Central Intelligence Agency, "GDP (Official Exchange Rate)," 6 May 2012, https://www.cia.gov/library/publications/the-world-factbook/fields/2195.html (accessed 6 May 2012).

Secondarily, the seven chosen assessment tools plus joint-training with internal security forces, the author is giving them scoring them dependent upon their expertise with each. Looking first at Adaptability, the reasoning behind the scoring is that an army which has had a wide variety of roles will likely be able to handle the uncertainty that comes with sudden battle. Readiness is a look at how quickly and efficiently the military is likely to react upon being given orders. Jane's World Armies' analysis provides a narrative description of the armies and how much they are attached to life in the garrison as well as how they might see readiness as a challenge for sudden operations. Deployment, Tasks, and Operations speaks to how the militaries are currently used and if they are deployed outside the country. This assessment takes into consideration experience in working with other countries and other doctrines, such as NATO or the UN Peacekeeping Forces.

Command and Control is very much directed at how the troops receive their orders and how those orders are implemented and assessed. Location of the headquarters and commanders as well as communication packages are also considered under this assessment. For Demographics, the scoring is determined on whether a military is conscript, volunteer, a mix of both, and whether foreign forces serve alongside host nation forces. An all-volunteer force rates a higher score than a conscription force but all of the forces have either foreigners within their military forces, whose loyalty might be stretched in battle, and/or forces which were tribally pledged to the king rather than to the country. These forces' loyalty may be challenged when a new ruler takes the throne or if their tribes remove their allegiance to the current ruler.

Morale is difficult to measure but for the countries where assessment is possible, morale is an indicator of how well troops may work together before a battle begins. Professionalism bespeaks to the officers and enlisted ability to complete their job to the best of their ability. It also lends itself to a code of professional ethos within the military.

The last item is Joint Training with Security Forces and is particularly vital to the countries in question. GCC countries are normally defensively postured against external threats and, as such, the security forces within each country are considered a secondary source of manpower, materiel, and method in protecting the local populace. In the unique case of Bahrain in March 2011, the PSF was called in to supplant the security forces already in place as well as the Bahraini military. Numbers of security forces are provided in the first table of this section but the score here is given based on how well the military and security forces work together. This is the most likely future course of action although, as in the case of Bahrain, it may be that PSF troops will be working with other countries' security forces rather than the militaries themselves.

The scoring is as follows: 1 = LOW, 2 = MEDIUM, and 3 = HIGH. The higher the score, the greater the capacity for the criteria and the better suited the military will be for deployment in an integrated GCC operation.

Table 4.   Military Assessment Matrix

	Adaptability	Readiness	Deployment Tasks, Operations	Command & Control	Demographics	Morale	Professionalism	Joint Training w/Security Forces	Total Score w/o Morale & Profession alism
KSA	1	1	2	1	2	1	1	2	9
UAE	3	3	2	1	2	n/a	2	2	13
Oman	3	2	2	1	2	3	3	2	12
Kuwait	2	2	2	2	1	n/a	2	2	11
Qatar	3	2	3	2	2	n/a	n/a	2	14
Bahrain	2	3	2	2	2	2	2	3	14
Morocco	1	2	2	2	2	1	2	2	11
Jordan	3	3	3	3	2	3	3	3	17

Source: Created by author. Based on information provided in Jane's World Armies for the eight countries. Morale and Professionalism assessments were not available for all countries.

Jordan demonstrates strong military capabilities when compared and contrasted to the GCC countries and Morocco. Although Morocco did not score as high as Jordan, it fared well in comparison to the largest GCC country, Saudi Arabia. Morocco's lowest scores, in Adaptability and Morale, can be seen as due in part to its stagnant mission along the southern border, limited ability to cross-train with other countries, as well as its economic limitations in providing for its troops. Cross-training within the GCC can provide some relief for these issues while increased economic investments may also translate into more modern equipment that can compliment, but not supplement, the PSF's own stock of materiel.

Lacking within the GCC's military scheme for the PSF is a publicized or recognized overarching doctrine for land war. Again, the PSF is based on ground forces integration and even though there was a naval coalition of sorts that turned back two Iranian 'supply' ships that tried to assist the Bahraini protesters[25] the thrust of the PSF is its land component. Integration with security forces is the standard for most of the GCC countries, especially in the aftermath of the Iraqi invasion of Kuwait and subsequent attack on Kuwait's oil infrastructure. That lesson, of infrastructure vulnerabilities, was not lost on any of the six who have hundreds of miles of pipeline, with natural gas and oil flowing through areas that are often not secured and very isolated. The key operations that are joint are often associated with infrastructure protection, hence the claim that Bahrain requested PSF assistance in March 2011 to "protect government facilities."[26]

Integration with security forces and other military forces is dependent upon a Command, Control, Communications, Computers, Intelligence, Surveillance (C4ISR) and Reconnaissance package which is completely lacking within the GCC. Within the assessment matrix half of the GCC scored Low for Command and Control while the other half scored Medium. A significant reason for this scoring is how the command structure within each country is organized. The commands tend to be, on paper at least, very centralized high up within the Executive branch. In countries where troops are separated by vast expanses of desert this can be problematic without a well-integrated method of communicating upper to lower ranks and vice versa. Without a communications piece, the Command and Control portion travels only one way with limited results when the situation on the ground changes and the local command is required to wait for orders.

Jordan stands as the sole country with a C4ISR package[27] for its land forces. That fact may entice others to have the benefit of testing it without procuring it. Morocco could also be exposed to the C4ISR package but it is not clear if Morocco would be in the position to purchase such a system, considering the cost. The lack of a C4ISR package for the GCC is a key restraint on developing the six countries integration, let alone eight countries. Without it, operations will be constrained by whatever communications package is in the area, dependent upon what area troops are deployed.

The Command piece is one that the Saudis try to control but, situation dependent, this is the one piece that they might consider passing to a more suitable and better trained country, i.e. Jordan. Both invitees have multinational experience with UN Peacekeeping Operations but only Jordan has regular multinational exercises with the UK military as well as other forces and is considered to be the most professional and able military within the Arab military spectrum.[28]

Economic

The economic agreement that binds the GCC together is based on a combination of trade, monetary regulations, investments, integrated developments, natural resources, manpower, and science and technology.[29] The foundation, though, of the agreement is the fact that the six countries have an abundance of natural resources and those resources are the source of their respective wealth. This wealth is a far cry from the two invitees who, while being the only other Sunni monarchies in the Arab world, suffer from a dearth of those same natural resources and rely on foreign economic assistance, whether by other countries or remittances from their own citizens. Jordan especially is considered natural resource deficient and is 'water poor', a country that has very little water access for its people.[30] Morocco relies on its agricultural sector more than any natural resource for a discernible portion of its Gross Domestic Product (GDP).[31]

The GCC countries are all categorized as wealthy by the International Monetary Fund while Jordan and Morocco are without question not as wealthy by far (see table 5). The GCC's charter lays out its economic expectations for the citizens of the group. Among them are that each country will try to diversify its economic outputs while ensuring that its citizenry is taken care of and educated at a high standard. This indicates a strategy of increasing the education of its people and seeking to increase the economic development of its countries. The benefits to the citizenry are wrapped in Islamic tradition where philanthropy is taught and expected, both on the governmental and individual level.

Table 5.   Country GDP Per Capita in U.S. Dollars

Source: Central Intelligence Agency, "The World Factbook:Economy: GDP Per Capita," 2011, https://www.cia.gov/library/publications/the-world-factbook/geos (accessed 12 April 2012). Figures are all estimates based on previous years' figures.

Where Morocco and Jordan may not be able to provide as well for their citizenry at the moment, they both can serve to assist in diversifying the GCC's petroleum and natural gas-centric portfolios. Both countries export clothing, fertilizers, and phosphates while Morocco also exports electric components and produce[32] and both have a vast pool of manpower in need of greater employment (see table 6). This is a key point within the GCC's own discussion for economic development as an influx of Arab workers would remove the concern that the GCC has over foreign workers.[33]

Table 6.   Citizen Unemployment within the Eight Countries

Source: Central Intelligence Agency, "The World Factbook: Country: Economy," 2012, https://www.cia.gov/library/publications/the-world-factbook/geos/ (accessed 12 April 2012). Oman, Kuwait, and Bahrain are estimates from 2004 (x2) and 2005.

The GDP per capita reflected in table 5 show that Jordan and Morocco, with figures of less than $10,000 USD trail far behind most of the GCC. But even within the

GCC there is the case of Qatar which has one of the highest GDPs per capita in the world. Qatar, with its very small population and geographical location has a figure of over $100,000 USD,[34] a figure that is also a source of envy within the GCC itself. The GDP figures stand as a source of leverage within the GCC, as to how equal the partners may be when they discuss topics for agreement. The GDP of Qatar offers the country a larger amount of influence than its size would seem to suggest.

The challenge for the focus on education for the GCC may lay with Morocco. The literacy figures for the GCC and Jordan are high, with all seven countries having 87 percent literacy rate or more for their respective populations. When one turns to Morocco the situation is very different. With a literacy rate of only 56 percent there is an organic challenge to raising the education level and skilled manpower level as well.

Table 7.   Adult Literacy Rates by Country

Source: World Bank, "Literacy Rate–Adult Total," http://data.worldbank.org/ indicator/SE.ADT.LITR.ZS:2011 (accessed 4 February 2012); "Government of UAE Website," 12 July 2010, http://www.uae-embassy.org/uae-us-relations/social-cultural (accessed 25 March 2012).

This, combined with Morocco's low GDP per capita and high unemployment rate, suggests that Morocco may provide the biggest challenges but also may benefit the most from entering the GCC. The GCC recognizes both Jordan and Morocco as having more financial stress than itself and has already pledged millions in grants to help develop their economic sector. Saudi Arabia was reported to have given Jordan a $400 million dollar grant[35] and there was discussion that during the GCC meeting in September 2011 the figure of $2 billion dollars per country per year for economic aid and development over the next five years was under consideration.[36]

Lastly, the inclusion of Jordan and Morocco will double the population size of the GCC and increase its total GDP by over ten percent. The invitation creates an imbalance wherein more than half of the GCC will now be from outside its geographical core area, namely the Arabian Gulf. The cultural impact remains to be seen and measured but just by sheer force of numbers there will be a change in the economic diversity of the GCC and its commercial ties and trade opportunities.

Table 8.   2010 Population By Country

Source: World Bank, "World Development Indicators by Country," 2011, WorldBank.org, http://databank.worldbank.org/Data/Views/Reports/TableView.aspx? IsShared=true&IsPopular=series (accessed 4 February 2012).

Morocco's main trading partners are Spain and France, and its trade with them is an anomaly within the context of the other seven countries. Those seven trade more heavily with Asia (India and China), the U.S., and amongst themselves,[37] but have a very small portion of their trade with Europe.

The impact of increased trading opportunities coupled with the increase in regional (GCC+2) manpower will result in re-circulating monies within the eight countries and subsequently increasing their GDPs. To what extent will be dependent upon how many Jordanians and Moroccans take up work within the GCC itself, but looking at one group of third-country nationals and what they remit back home gives a sample of the how the economies of Jordan and Morocco could be impacted. In 2011 the

Central Bank of the Philippines tracked remittances from all countries of origin. Within that one year for the six GCC countries, the remittances totaled $233 million dollars.[38] This does not include monies that may have been carried back personally by the workers but gives a picture of how much money is being moved between the countries by the mostly unskilled laborers. That type of figure is substantial in areas of Morocco and Jordan where there is high unemployment or underemployment and would increase the economic prospects of those same areas.

R-DIME Analysis for the Eight

In looking at the information and data, the grouping of the eight countries can be analyzed by assessing their ability to integrate using the following matrix. For the countries who can integrate with the two invitees the letter "C" will represent a cooperative environment, meaning that the countries should be able to incorporate the new members within each sector with ease. For the countries which are dissimilar within the instruments of power the letter "D" will represent a disjointed environment. The dissimilarity will cause a challenge for the new countries to blend in within the particular sectors, whether due to ideology within the sector (as is possible with military practice) or with national programs (as in financial sector planning which focuses on debt reduction, a situation the GCC does not face).

69

Table 9.   R-DIME Integration Assessment of the GCC, Jordan, and Morocco

	RELIGION	DIPLOMATIC	INFORMATION	MILITARY	ECONOMIC
KSA	C	C	C	C	C
UAE	C	C	C	C	C
OMAN	C	C	C	C	C
KUWAIT	C	C	C	C	C
QATAR	C	C	C	C	C
BAHRAIN	C	C	C	C	D
MOROCCO	C	C	C	C	D
JORDAN	C	C	C	C	D

Source: Created by author. *R-DIME Integration Assessment of the GCC countries with Jordan and Morocco* (April 2012).

The matrix shows congruence among the religion/governance, diplomatic, information, and military abilities within the eight countries. In reaching back to Chapter 2 which outlined the respective governments' establishment, how each country has diplomatic relations either within the GCC or as Arab nations outside the GCC, with each other and with other international governmental organizations, how each country controls the flow and type of information within its borders, and how defense of its borders is considered essential to the GCC's existence, the similarities among them are clear. The key differences lie within the economic realm where the two invitees have GDPs that are, at best, one fifth of the next-closest country. The differences also with Morocco's low literacy rate indicate a poorer education system which is tied to a lack of economic spending in the educational sector.

The economic sector is where the disjointed environment stands out in from the other assessment factors. Within the economic sector the two invitees are most dissimilar to the GCC and the GCC may have to assist the two in developing their economic capabilities in order to achieve full integration with them. There is no minimum GDP for the GCC but the original six countries are tied to the natural fuel resources originating from their geographical area; namely oil and gas. Morocco and Jordan may not have the same resources but GCC can integrate the two by developing alternate trade and development projects for them and increasing their GDP by hiring their unemployed to work within the GCC. Increasing Arab employment would benefit the eight countries across-the-board and expedite integration into the GCC for Jordan and Morocco.

Up Ahead

The analysis of the R-DIME instruments of power, within the parameters that were used, shows that there are clear military benefits to the inclusion of Jordan and Morocco into the GCC as well as some economic challenges to the inclusion as well. The military benefits would include the greater professionalism that is found within the Jordanian military and security forces as well as the sheer number of Moroccan troops that could be trained for deployment within the Arabian Gulf area. Economically, there are challenges in integrating the poorer invitees but they offer a unique benefit in that their trade partners are unlike the ones the GCC is accustomed to. Using the information and data that was presented in this chapter, the final chapter will conclude with the

71

narrative synthesis of the response to the primary and secondary questions as well as

make recommendations for further research into the subject

---

[1]Ms. Andrea Gastaldo, personal experience as an officer within the U.S. Embassy in Riyadh (1998-2000).

[2]"Saudi Arabia–Constitution," March 1992, http://www.servate.unibe.ch/icl/sa00000_.html (accessed 15 March 2012); "UAE– onstitution," 2 December 1971, http://www.uaecabinet.ae/English/UAEGovernment/Pages/constitution_1_1.aspx, (accessed 25 March 2012); "Oman–Constitution," 6 November 1996, http://www.servat.unibe.ch/icl/mu00000_.html(accessed 25 March 2012); "Kuwait– onstitution," 11 November 1962, http://www.servat.unibe.ch/icl/ku00000_.html (accessed 25 March 2012); "Qatar–Constitution," 2 July 2 2002, http://www.qataembassy.net/constitution.asp (accessed 19 March 2012); "Bahrain–Constitution," 14 February 2002, http://www.servat.unibe.ch/icl/ba00000_.html (accessed 16 April 2012); "Morocco–Constitution," 13 September 1996, http://www.al-bab.com/maroc/gov/con96.htm (accessed 16 April 2012); "Jordan–Constitution," as amended 1 September 1984, http://www.kinghussein.gov.jo/const_ch1-9.html (accessed 16 April 2012); Berne University, Governments of UAE, Qatar, Morocco, Jordan.

[3]"Saudi Arabia–Constitution," 1.

[4]"Qatar–Constitution," 1.

[5]"UAE–Constitution"; "Morocco–Constitution."

[6]"Kuwait–Constitution."

[7]United Nations, "UN at a Glance," http://www.un.org/en/aboutun/index.shtml (accessed 4 February 2012).

[8]General Secretariat of the League of Arab States, "Member States," League of Arab States, http://www.arableagueonline.org/wps/portal/las_en/inner/!ut/p/c5/ (accessed 6 February 2012).

[9]Matt Bradley and Charles Levinson, "Wall Street Journal Online," *Wall Street Journal,* http://online.wsj.com/article/SB10001424052748704838804576196681609529882.html (accessed 10 November 2011).

[10]Ibid.

[11]Patrick J. McDonnell, "Los Angeles Times Online," *Los Angeles Times,* http://latimesblogs.latimes.com/world_now/2011/11/syria-arab-league-suspension.html (accessed 3 April 2012).

[12]The Cooperation Council for the Arab States of the Gulf Secretariat General, "The Revised Long-Term Comprehensive Development Strategy for the GCC States 2010-2025," Gulf Cooperation Council, http://sites.gcc-sg.org/DLibrary/index-eng.php?action=New (accessed 12 April 2012).

[13]International Court of Justice, "Maritime Delimitation and Territorial Questions between Qatar and Bahrain (Qatar vs. Bahrain)," September 2001, International Court of Justice, http://www.icj-cij.org/common/print.php?pr=234&pt=1&p1=6&p2=1 (accessed 20 March 2012).

[14]Israeli Ministry of Foreign Affairs, "Israel's Diplomatic Missions Abroad: Status of Relations," September 2011, http://www.mfa.gov.il/MFA/About+the+Ministry/ Diplomatic+missions/Israel-s+Diplomatic+Missions+Abroad.htm (accessed 4 February 2012).

[15]Freedom House.org, "2011 Freedom of the Press Data," 2011, http://www.freedomhouse.org/report-types/freedom-press (accessed 20 April 2012).

[16]Economic Affairs, Commerce and Industry Department, *The Revised Long-Term Development Strategy for the GCC States 2010-2025* (Riyadh, Saudi Arabia: Gulf Cooperation Council, 2011), 28.

[17]Saudi Press Agency, "Saudi Arabia Opens New Facility for Peninsula Shield Force," 2 December 2003, Saudi News Agency, http://lumen.cgsccarl.com/login?url= http://proquest.umi.com/pqdweb?did=472048591&Fmt=3&clientId=5094&RQT=309& VName=PQD (accessed 16 November 2011).

[18]GlobalSecurity.org, "Military: Gulf Cooperation Council," http://www. globalsecurity.org/military/world/gulf/gcc.htm (accessed 9 December 2011).

[19]Tawazun Holdings, "Military and Sporting Weapons," 2011, Tawazun, http://www.tawazun.ae/en/our-subsidiaries/military-and-sporting-weapons.aspx (accessed April 17, 2012).

[20]Jane's Defense & Intelligence Analysis, "Jane's World Armies-Jordan," 27 June 2011, http://jwar.janes.com/subscribe/jwar/doc_view_print.jsp?K2DocKey=content1/ janesdata/bi (accessed 2 February 2012), 2.

[21]Jane's Defense & Intelligence Analysis, "Jane's Sentinel Security Assessment, Executive Summary, Jordan at a Glance," 18 July 2011, http://sentinel.janes.com/ subscribe/sentinel/doc_view_print.jsp?K2DocKey=/content1/janes (accessed 16 September 2011), 3.

[22]Jane's Defense & Intelligence Analysis, "Jane's World Armies-Morocco," 3 November 2011, http://jwar.janes.com/subscribe/jwar/doc_view_print.jsp?K2DocKey=/content1/janesdata/bi (accessed 4 February 2012), 7.

[23]Jane's Defense & Intelligence Analysis, "Jane's World Armies–UAE," 7 November 2011, http://jwar.janes.com/subscribe/jwar/doc_view_print.jsp?K2DocKey=/content1/janesdata/bi (accessed 4 Febraury 2012).

[24]Central Intelligence Agency, "The World Factbook–GCC Countries plus Jordan and Morocco," https://www.cia/gov/library/publications/the-world-factbook/geos/countrytemplate (accessed 12 April 2012).

[25]Thomas Erdbrink, "Iranian Ships Carrying Aid to Bahrain Turned Back in Persian Gulf," *Washington Post,* 16 May 2011, http://www.washingtonpost.com/world/iranian-ships-carrying-aid-to-bahrain-turned-back-in-persian-gulf/2011/05/16/AFho954G_story.html (accessed 14 November 2011).

[26]"Peninsula Shield Forces Enter Bahrain to Maintain Order," *Asharq Al Awsat Newspaper,* 15 March 2011, http://www.asharq-e.com/news.asp?section=1&id=24509 (accessed 17 September 2011).

[27]Jane's Defense & Intelligence Analysis, "Jane's Sentinel Security Assessment, Executive Summary, Jordan at a Glance."

[28]Ibid, 1.

[29]The Cooperation Council for the Arab States of the Gulf Secretariat General, "The Economic Agreement," 31 December 2001, Gulf Cooperation Council, http://library.gcc-sg.org/English/Books/econagree2004.htm (accessed 31 October 2011), 3-6.

[30]Department of State, "Background Note: Jordan," 30 December 2011, Bureau of Near East Affairs, http://www.state.gov/r/pa/ei/bgn/3464.htm (accessed 4 February 2012).

[31]Department of State, "Background Note: Morocco," 12 March 2012, Bureau of Near Eastern Affairs, http://www.state.gov/r/pa/ei/bgn/5431.htm (accessed 26 March 2012).

[32]Central Intelligence Agency, "Africa: Morocco: Economy: Industries," 23 February 2012, https://www.cia.gov/library/publications/the-world-factbook/geos/countrytemplate_mo.html (accessed 12 April 2012); Central Intelligence Agency, "Middle East: Jordan: Economy: Industries," 22 March 2012, https://www.cia.gov/library/publications/the-world-factbook/geos/countrytemplate_jo.html, (accessed 12 April 2012).

[33]The Cooperation Council for the Arab States of the Gulf Secretariat General, "The Revised Long-Term Comprehensive Development Strategy for the GCC States 2010-2025,"Gulf Cooperation Council, http://sites.gcc-sg.org/DLibrary/index-eng.php?action=New (accessed 12 April 2012), 12.

[34]Central Intelligence Agency, "Middle East: Qatar: Economy: GDP Per Capita," 20 March 2012, https://www.cia/gov/library/publications/the-world-factbook/geos/countrytemplate_qa.html (accessed 12 April 2012).

[35]Anne Allemeling and Johannes Krug, "Analysis: How Jordan and Morocco Change the Gulf Cooperation Council," 9 June 2011, Al Arabiya, http://english.alarabiya.net/articles/2011/06/09/152623.html (accessed 6 April 2012).

[36]David Schenker, "The Cutting Edge," 12 October 2011, The Washington Institute, http://www.thecuttingedgenews.com/index.php?article=52902&pageid=&pagename= (accessed 6 April 2012).

[37]Central Intelligence Agency, "The World Factbook–GCC Countries plus Jordan and Morocco."

[38]Central Bank of the Philippines, "Overseas Filipinos' Remittances-Bangko Sentral ng Pilipinas," 11-12.

CHAPTER 5

CONCLUSION

In considering the information presented in the previous chapters and looking at the countries under discussion, the general statement can be made that the two invitees are much more similar to the GCC countries than they are discordant. The unification of the Sunni monarchies, or Arab monarchies if you will since there are no Shia monarchies within the Arab world, seems to be a natural evolvement in light of the threats that surround their continued existence. The GCC's reason d'être, as an economic bloc as well as a unifying entity to counter the threat of an encroaching Iran, is still valid but the six countries now face varying levels of domestic discord since February 2011. The two invitees have also hosted their share of protests but at a much lower level, with the issue of reform at the center rather than the issue of leadership.

The congruence within four of the five instruments of national power indicates that integration within these four instruments should not create challenges for the GCC since the eight countries are on the same page as far as the method and implementation of them. In the context of Religion and Governance conjointly, there should be little impact in integrating the invitees into the GCC as their way of government, not simply as monarchies but more fundamentally in the rule of law, the eight countries have very little variation. How the legal system is run within the GCC is basically how it is run in Jordan and Morocco. The strict Wahhabi interpretation of Saudi Arabia is not contradictory to how the law is implemented in other GCC countries but it pushes the law into a social context for every public and private situation. Again, the strict interpretation is well-known and does not contradict the method in which the government is run, in comparison

76

to the other seven. The Saudi legal system's application of judicial punishment is well-known and accepted as just within the GCC. The invitees' citizenry will be held accountable under the legal system of any of the six GCC countries and as they are considered to be in accordance with Islam they should not be an issue for contention.

On the Diplomatic front the eight countries seem to share comparable outlooks on a diverse range of topics. The issue often raised within the GCC minutes, that being concern over Iran's nuclear program and aspirations,[1] is not one raised in Morocco but one expects that the two invitees will agree on the GCC diplomatic platform once they are accorded full member status. The Jordanian decision to send fighter jets to Libya in July 2011,[2] after Qatar had done the same, can be viewed as a first step in moving closer to adopting the GCC's diplomatic line of action. Although the use of fighter jets is often seen as a military action, the decision to send them required a coordinated diplomatic effort with advance agreement of the countries to be overflown as well as any other forces in the area in order to avoid any friendly-fire incidents.

In addition to the internal diplomatic impact, wherein the GCC plus two will likely gel into a cohesive unit that will have a larger voice within the Arab League and UN, there is also the external approach from other countries that may be impacted. The U.S. Department of State places Jordan and Morocco within the same diplomatic realm based on their place within the Arab world so there would be minimal change in its diplomatic approach. But the Department of State works closely with the Department of Defense on issues such as Status of Forces Agreements, overflight permissions, and basing requests with host nation governments. Currently Jordan is within the CENTCOM area of responsibility but Morocco is not, due to the fact that it lies in Africa. The inclusion of Morocco into the GCC and the use of the GCC countries as friendly countries for basing require the Department of Defense rethink Morocco's current geographic grouping. If CENTCOM is to fully synchronize its deployment of forces in the area for strategic effect within a "security architecture,"[3] the future use of Morocco as a staging area for the Arabian Gulf area of responsibility should force either a joint-casting of Morocco into both AFRICOM and CENTCOM's portfolio or a hybrid.

This is a complicated issue and one that may be resolved by having AFRICOM and CENTCOM liaise specifically on Morocco while keeping it in one or the other's portfolio. It should be noted that a shift of Morocco from AFRICOM to CENTCOM will likely have strategic implications for the GCC itself and may be viewed by others, namely Iran, as focusing on the GCC's military capabilities above its economic interests and capacities. That, in and of itself, may create a cause for concern as it will raise the GCC's military standing and possibly increase the regional tension already present.

The monarchies outlook on Information and the media are quite close and because of that, there is likelihood that control of the media will either remain the same or intensify as the state-sponsored media outlets begin reading off the same sheet of music from eight countries rather than six. There is a greater risk though also associated with the two new countries. That would be the inherent risk of the instant social media, Twitter and the like, which are hard to censor due to the speed in which they broadcast their messages. The news that the GCC invited Jordan and Morocco to the group was initially broke on Twitter and flashed through the Arab world within minutes, not hours.[4] The GCC will double in size once the invitations turn into membership and that will equate into a vast increase in the blogging and Twittering that will occur. Although the

Moroccan and Jordanian media have some constraints on criticizing their respective monarchs that does not translate into the same media holding back on other countries' monarchs.

That creates a greater risk that the GCC countries, and specifically their leaders, will come under media attack from a population that will be difficult to counter. The Moroccan bloggers in particular had some hesitant and negative comments for the GCC upon news of the invitations. Morocco does not share the same intermingling with the GCC that Jordan has so it would make sense to assume that Moroccans may be more tepid and questioning about the membership as compared to Jordan.

The military attributes of each country vary, but the one item that the GCC countries lack is true integration. There is currently limited organic ability to cross-train within the GCC and the military leadership within the PSF is not open about its forces' ability to counter anything more than civil disobedience.[5] The inclusion of Jordan should be seen as a huge plus to the PSF and, if allowed to lead the training, should result in a more integrated force and measureable standard of capability that is currently lacking for the PSF overall.

Morocco's ability to impact the PSF will be entirely dependent upon sending troops to train with GCC equipment. As Morocco not only has the oldest equipment but is also more reliant upon French equipment that is not in the other countries' arsenals, it will take some time for the Moroccans to get up to speed on training in the mostly U.S./UK MBTs and other heavier equipment that do not exist within the Maghrebi inventory. There are older M60s and T-72s that Morocco uses but if Morocco is to add troop numbers to the PSF and be used as an effective fighting force they will have to be trained and trained on the equipment that they will be using. That will require time away from their own military as well as extended efforts to create a modular Moroccan unit (battalion or brigade size likely) that can be familiarized with the GCC methods of operation and terrain.

Jordan does not have as significant a challenge integrating since there are Jordanian trainers within the GCC who understand the military design of the PSF and of the individual countries themselves. There are also Jordanians serving in the GCC militaries as officers and enlisted who can provide a knowledge-based pool of the GCC's methods of operation.

Externally, the GCC's allies may want to consider this inclusion as an opportunity to review how the GCC has equipped itself and whether or not a comprehensive military fitness plan might be of use. The mélange of equipment will likely be less than optimally effective in a defensive fight when using an assortment of troops from various military backgrounds and doctrines.

This leads to a key point. If the GCC's PSF does not create a combined arms doctrine that can take into account the customarily joint doctrine precepts of Doctrine, Organization, Training, Materiel, Leadership, Personnel, and Facilities capacities, then it will not be able to evolve into an effective fighting force and will have to continually rely on its allies, namely the U.S., for assistance and support. The inclusion of Jordan and Morocco can help boost numbers and expertise but it cannot replace sound doctrine and integration. Joint forces also should be considered at the same time as the land war component if the joint forces are to be integrated into the mutual defense pact.

Economically, the impact on the GCC and the two invitees will be the most substantial of all five elements of national power. On the one hand the inclusion of the two countries whose GDP is substantially lower than the other six can negatively impact the economic bloc if their economic diversity is not exploited. On the other hand, the two can provide a widening of trade relations with countries not normally associated with the GCC. The industries of each invitee provide an opportunity for the GCC to look beyond their petroleum/gas based futures into something that may endure after their current reserves are diminished and are no longer viable for export. The reserves of Kuwait, for example, can be expected to diminish drastically in as little as 30 years. This is the reality that the GCC is facing and economic diversification is one of the goals of the organization. Morocco and Jordan may help them find the answers to other exports and other sources of output. Jordan's military industry, albeit fledgling, may hold an answer with the right influx of research and development.

That the GCC is taking an economic chance on these two countries should not be a surprise since the GCC emerged from countries that were considered 'dirt poor' only sixty years ago. The combination of the governmental, cultural, and social aspects makes the inclusion a sensible idea. The added fact that the GCC would like to lessen the number of foreign workers makes the invitation very logical, if the new members will add their manpower to work in the GCC's gulf economies. The use of Jordanian and Moroccan manpower will increase the general wealth of those two countries and will serve to strengthen the ties between all eight. The remittances back home spent within the two countries will serve to boost their respective economies while the training that the new employment immigrants receive will help the two countries raise their education levels.

As to the timing of the invitations, that can be considered to be the result of a combination of political and fortuitous events. The GCC, as any large organization with powerful members, does not make decisions quickly and without logic. The membership of Jordan had already been under consideration in the past although there are disputed accounts as to whether or not Jordan had been refused in the past or it had never requested consideration. The fact is that the Sunni monarchs all know each other and are all aware of each other's strengths and weaknesses. There are not so many of them that they can ignore where each of them succeeds and fails. The decision to invite may have been precipitated by the uprisings within the Arab world but their roots are more likely to have been based on the requirement to withdraw of American troops from Iraq in mid-2010 and the understanding that the focus of American and other allies' strength would be in Afghanistan only until 2014. Discord and infighting within the region is not a new occurrence but the drawdown of a significant amount of Western troops after more than a decade of close cooperation required the monarchs to rethink how they positioned themselves.

The timing was fortuitous because the announcement, catching most of the media and public by surprise, had the effect of seeming to be in response to the Bahraini uprising and the ouster of Tunisia and Egypt's Presidents and led many to believe that it was more of a military move than an economic one. The fact is that there could be no mass movement of Moroccan troops without some sort of advance planning, evidence of which could not be found. The Jordanian addition adds expertise and professionalism but not actually large numbers of military troops, so the effect on the ground would be limited in the immediate timeframe. The unconfirmed numbers of Jordanian security forces that were sent to Bahrain did play a part but the denial of their existence within the country downplayed the perception that Jordan was involved with the GCC.

Full and Future Impact

When viewing the massive financial wealth of the GCC plus two, together with the increase in manpower that Morocco and Jordan would bring to a military operation, one could consider that the new GCC could become a military powerhouse in the Arabian Gulf region. That consideration, though, needs to be scrutinized in the light of each country's assessed capabilities as listed within the matrix in table 4. The countries each bring assets to the military table but the lack of integration amongst the whole group is a glaring omission in strategy and the key to what will hamstring the PSF in a military operation.

There is no history of combined training with all six countries, whether that is land forces or joint training with air and sea elements. There is also no demonstrated capacity to host more than a brigade at a time within the PSF HQ in Saudi Arabia. The inclusion of Morocco and Jordan may, in the future, increase the military capability of the PSF but this increase can only be considered effective with concerted training, the creation of a PSF doctrine that all countries can incorporate within their home training, and with synchronization of the C4ISR package which is currently non-existent. The wealth of the richest countries allows them the latitude to purchase the latest equipment and hire contractors to maintain and train military on them but this does not equate into creating a viable and integrated fighting force. For the PSF to become a military powerhouse will require the command and control of the organization to be based on professionalism rather than relying on the bill payer. Additionally, the PSF will have to begin combined training with all eight countries participating at battalion and brigade level strength as well as joint training, once the combined training has reached a level of proficiency that will permit effective joint training to occur.

The addition of these two countries into the GCC has not been finalized and the impact of their inclusion will only be completely evaluated after a transition period wherein the two are fully integrated into all that the GCC has to offer. The question of what the inclusion means to the GCC as well as to the U.S. is answered only in the short term as full membership needs to occur before all of the pieces of this development fall into place and the new GCC can be seen and understood. Full membership can still be years away. The immediate impact can be seen in the inclusion of the Jordanian security forces during Bahrain's demonstrations and, farther down the line, the employment of Moroccans and Jordanians in greater numbers in the GCC. The use of the Jordanian military and Moroccan military will require integration with the PSF that will be challenging due to its lack of doctrine and command and control structure.

Should the integration with the military and economic elements ever be completed and should the PSF become a cohesive and integrated security force, the GCC would then be able to rely less upon its allies, specifically the U.S., and more upon itself. If the GCC does become more self-sufficient and less dependent upon others then the diplomatic dialogue with the U.S. and other allies will likely change to take into consideration its military maturity and capability. That self-sufficiency, even with the two invitees, is not yet on the horizon and needs more time to develop, form, and be tested.

For the moment, the relationship with the U.S. will likely remain unaltered and the majority of military support for the GCC countries will continue to be from its allies.

As to what the GCC itself sees itself becoming, the official reports continue to focus on its economic intent and little else. There is contextual information on how it sees itself as a protector of its citizens and its firm belief that education is vital for the countries to continue to develop but the group's future intent is still not clear. Further research into this inclusion as it unfolds and after the two countries are participatory members will serve to better understand the GCC's intent and its possible future capabilities. Specifically on the military aspect of the GCC, further study into the PSF and its command and control structure and the politics behind it will serve to better understand how it can and cannot be used if the GCC is threatened.

Lastly, the U.S., by including the GCC as a group that it sees itself working with, has a vested interest in how the GCC prepares and plans for its future. Its military aspect is of great import but it hinges on the continued economic growth within the GCC and continued diplomatic rapport with its neighbors. Iran is keenly aware of the issue of inclusion and even put out a disinformation piece stating that the invitations had been withdrawn,[6] while Israel also has kept tabs on the developments; several pieces in the Israeli press raise the invitation as a question of concern for future relations with Jordan.[7]

Whatever the outcome, the inclusion into the GCC of Jordan and Morocco is no small bit of news and should not be discounted if it does come to fruition. It has been more than a hundred years since the world has last seen a monarchal grouping of countries. The GCC plus two would represent a grouping of countries that with training and integration could become a military force of limited effect, but an economic and

diplomatic bloc of enduring influence.

---

[1]Gulf Cooperation Council, "The Final Communiqué of the 30th Session: The Iranian Nuclear Dossier," July 2009, http://www.gcc-sg.org/eng/indexce7c.html?action=Sec-Show&ID=303 (accessed 15 November 2012).

[2]Jane's Defense & Intelligence Analysis, "Jane's Sentinel Country Risk Assessments-Air Force, Jordan," 12 August 2011, http://sentinel.janes.com/subscribe/sentinel/doc_view_print.jsp?K2DocKey=/content1/jane (accessed 16 September 2011), 3.

[3]Thom Shanker and Steven Lee Myers, "U.S. Planning Troop Buildup in Gulf after Exit from Iraq," *New York Times,* 30 October 2011, http://www.nytimes.com/2011/10/30/world/middleeast/united-states-plans-post-iraq-troop-increase-in-persian-gulf.html?_r=1&pagewanted=all (accessed 3 January 2012).

[4]Historum, "Jordan and Morocco to join GCC!!!" 10 May 2011, History Discussion Forum, http://www.historum.com/current-events-history-making/24507-jordan-morocco-join-gcc (accessed 5 October 2011).

[5]Muqbil Al-Saeri, "A Talk with Peninsula Shield Force Commander Mutlaq Bin Salem Al-Azima," *Asharq Alawsat* (28 March 2011), Bahrain.

[6]Sayyed Mohiyeddin Sajedi, "[P]GCC Overturns Membership Invitations," 4 December 2011, Iranian PressTV, http://www.presstv.ir/detail/213784.html (accessed 23 January 2012).

[7]Gavriel Queenann, "Jordan to Join the GCC in September," 8 August 2011, Arutz Sheva, Israel National News, http://israelnationalnews.com/news.news.aspx/146512 (accessed 5 October 2011).

BIBLIOGRAPHY

Books

Al-Hijji, Yacoub Y. *Old Kuwait: Memories in Photographs.* Kuwait: Center for Research and Studies on Kuwait, 2004.

Cordesman, Anthony H., and Nawaf Obaid. *National Security in Saudi Arabia.* Washington, DC: Praeger Security International Advisory Board, 2005.

Hackett, James Ed. *The Military Balance 2010.* London: Routledge, 2010.

Hazleton, Lesley. *After The Prophet: The Epic Story of the Shia Sunni Split in Islam.* New York, NY: Doubleday, 2009.

Pollack, Kenneth M. *Arabs At War, Military Effectiveness, 1948-1991.* Lincoln, NE: University of Nebraska Press, 2002.

Long, David E. and Christian Koch. *Gulf Security in the Twenty-First Century.* Abu Dhabi: The Emirates Center for Strategic Studies and Research, 1997.

Nydell, Margaret. *Understanding Arabs.* Yarmouth: Intercultural Press, 2006.

Rathmell, Andrew. *The Changing Military Balance in the Gulf.* London: RUSI Whitehall Paper Series, 1996.

Shirazi, Imam Muhammad. *The Islamic System of Government.* London: Fountain Books, 2002.

Terrill, Andrew W. *Kuwaiti National Security and the U.S.-Kuwaiti Strategic Relationship After Saddam.* Carlisle, PA: U.S.Army War College Strategic Studies Institute, 2007.

Wolcott, Harry F. *Writing Up Qualitative Research.* Los Angeles: SAGE Publications, 2009.

Government Documents

Department of the Army. Field Manual 3-0, *Operations.* Washington, DC: Government Printing Office, 2011.

_____. Field Manual 3-05, *Army Special Operations Forces Unconventional Warfare.* Washington, DC: Government Printing Office, 30 September 2008.

_____. Field Manual 1, *Army*. Washington, DC: Government Printing Office, June 2005.

Department of Defense. *Sustaining U.S. Global Leadership: Priorities for 21st Century Defense*. Washington, DC: Government Printing Office, 5 January 2012.

Economic Affairs, Commerce and Industry Department, *The Revised Long-Term Development Strategy for the GCC States 2010-2025*. Riyadh, Saudi Arabia: Gulf Cooperation Council, 2011.

Internet Sources

Al Jazeera. "Arab Monarchs Respond to Spreading Revolutions." http://www.aljazeerah. info/News/2011/May/11 percent20n/Arab percent20Monarchs percent20Respond percent20to percent20Spreading percent20Revolutions (accessed 26 September 2011).

Allemeling, Anne, and Johannes Krug. "Analysis: How Jordan and Morocco Change the Gulf Cooperation Council." Al Arabiya. http://english.alarabiya.net/articles/ 2011/06/09/152623.html (accessed 6 April 2012).

"Bahrain–Constitution." http://www.servat.unibe.ch/icl/ba00000_.html (accessed 16 April 2012).

Bahrain Freedom.org. "Bahrain Freedom Blog." http://bahrainfreedom.org/ (accessed 31 October 2011).

Bradley, Matt, and Charles Levinson. "Wall Street Journal Online." *Wall Street Journal*. http://online.wsj.com/article/SB10001424052748704838804576196681 609529882.html (accessed 10 November 2011).

Central Bank of the Philippines. "Overseas Filipinos' Remittances-Bangko Sentral ng Pilipinas." http://www.bsp.gov.ph/statistics/keystat/ofw.htm (accessed 13 March 2012).

Central Intelligence Agency. "Africa: Morocco: Economy: Industries." https://www.cia.gov/library/publications/the-world-factbook/geos/country template_mo.html (accessed 12 April 2012).

_____. "Middle East: Jordan: Economy: Industries." https://www.cia.gov/library/ publications/the-world-factbook/geos/countrytemplate_jo.html (accessed 12 April 2012).

_____. "Middle East: Qatar: Economy: GDP Per Capita." https://www.cia/gov/library/ publications/the-world-factbook/geos/countrytemplate_qa.html (accessed 12 April 2012).

_____. "The World Factbook: Africa: Morocco." https://www.cia.gov/library/publications/the-world-factbook/geos/mo.html (accessed 5 December 2011).

_____. "The World Factbook–GCC Countries plus Jordan and Morocco." https://www.cia/gov/library/publications/the-world-factbook/geos/countrytemplate (accessed 12 April 2012).

CNN Wire Staff. "Foreign Troops Enter Bahrain as Protests Continue." CNN. http://articles.cnn.com/2011-03-14/world/bahrain.protests_1_foreign -troops-bahraini-government-security-forc?_s=PM:WORLD (accessed 14 September 2011).

The Cooperation Council for the Arab States of the Gulf Secretariat General. "The Economic Agreement." Gulf Cooperation Council. http://library.gcc-sg.org/English/Books/econagree2004.htm (accessed 31 October 2011).

_____. "The Revised Long-Term Comprehensive Development Strategy for the GCC States 2010-2025." Gulf Cooperation Council. http://sites.gcc-sg.org/DLibrary/index-eng.php?action=New (accessed 12 April 2012).

Data Arabia. "Family Tree." http://www.datarabia.com/royals/home.do (accessed 5 April 2012).

Department of Commerce. "Free Trade Agreements." Office of the United States Trade Representative. http://www.ustr.gov/trade-agreements/free-trade-agreements (accessed 12 March 2012).

Department of State. "Background Note: Bahrain." Bureau of Near Eastern Affairs. http://www.state.gov/r/pa/ei/bgn/26414.htm (accessed 19 January 2012).

_____. "Background Note: Jordan." Bureau of Near Eastern Affairs. http://www.state.gov/r/pa/ei/bgn/3464.htm (accessed 19 January and 4 February 2012).

_____. "Background Note: Morocco." Bureau of African Affairs. http://www.state.gov/r/pa/ei/bgn/5431.htm (accessed 2 December 2011 and 26 March 2012).

_____. "Background Note: Oman." Bureau of Near Eastern Affairs. http://www.state.gov/r/pa/ei/bgn/35834.htm (accessed 12 January 2012).

_____. "Background Note: United Arab Emirates." Bureau of Near Eastern Affairs. http://www.state.gov/r/pa/ei/bgn/5444.htm (accessed 29 December 2011).

_____. "Saudi Arabia–Country Specific Requirements." http://travel.state.gov/travel/cis_pa_tw/cis/cis_1012.html#entry_requirements (accessed 5 December 2011).

Dubai Media Incorporated. "GCC GDP to Accelerate to 6.8 Percent in 2011." http://www.emirates247.com/business/economy-finance/gcc-gdp-to-accelerate-to-6-8-in-2011-2011-06-03-1.400707 (accessed 26 September 2011).

Embassy of State of Al Qatar. "History." http://www.qatarembassy.net/history.asp (accessed 19 March 2012).

Erdbrink, Thomas. "Iranian Ships Carrying Aid to Bahrain Turned Back in Persian Gulf." *Washington Post,* 16 May 2011. http://www.washingtonpost.com/world/iranian-ships-carrying-aid-to-bahrain-turned-back-in-persian-gulf/2011/05/16/AFho954G_story.html (accessed 14 November 2011).

Freedom House.org. "2011 Freedom of the Press Data." Freedom House. http://www.freedomhouse.org/report-types/freedom-press (accessed 20 April 2012).

General Secretariat of the League of Arab States. "Member States." League of Arab States. http://www.arableagueonline.org/wps/portal/las_en/inner/!ut/p/c5/ (accessed 6 February 2012).

GlobalSecurity.org. "Military: Gulf Cooperation Council." http://www.globalsecurity.org/military/world/gulf/gcc.htm (accessed 9 December 2011).

Government of Jordan. "The Hashemites." http://www.kingabdullah.jo/index.php/en_US/pages/view/id/220.html (accessed 27 March 2012).

_____. "The Hashemites–Early History." http://www.kingabdullah.jo/index.php/en_US/pages/view/id/157.html (accessed 27 March 2012).

Government of United Arab Emirates. "Constitution of UAE." http://www.uaecabinet.ae/English/UAEGovernment/Pages/constitution_1_4.aspx (accessed 25 March 2012).

_____. "UAE Federal National Council." http://www.uae-embassy.org/uae/government/federal-national-council (accessed 25 March 2012).

_____. "UAE Foreign Aid." http://ww.uae-embassy.org/uae/foreign-policy/foreign-aid. (accessed 25 March 2012).

Gulf Cooperation Council. "The Economic Agreement." http://library.gcc-sg.org/english/books/econagree2004.htm (accessed 31 October 2011).

_____. "The Final Communiqué of the 30th Session: The Iranian Nuclear Dossier." http://www.gcc-sg.org/eng/indexce7c.html?action=Sec-Show&ID=303 (accessed 15 November 2012).

_____. "Gulf Cooperation Council Charter." http://www.gcc-sg.org/eng/indexfc7a.html?action=SecShow&ID=1 (accessed 10 September 2011).

Historum. "Jordan and Morocco to join GCC!!!" History Discussion Forum. http://www.historum.com/current-events-history-making/24507-jordan-morocco-join-gcc (accessed 5 October 2011).

International Court of Justice. "Maritime Delimitation and Territorial Questions between Qatar and Bahrain (Qatar vs. Bahrain)." http://www.icj-cij.org/common/print.php?pr=234&pt=1&p1=6&p2=1 (accessed 20 March 2012).

International Monetary Fund. "IMF Country Information Page." http://www.imf.org/external/country/index.htm (accessed 4 February 2012).

Israeli Ministry of Foreign Affairs. "Israel's Diplomatic Missions Abroad: Status of Relations." http://www.mfa.gov.il/MFA/About+the+Ministry/Diplomatic+missions/Israel-s+Diplomatic+Missions+Abroad.htm (accessed 4 February 2012).

Jane's Defense & Intelligence Analysis. "Jane's Sentinel Country Risk Assessments-Air Force, Jordan." http://sentinel.janes.com/subscribe/sentinel/doc_view_print.jsp?K2DocKey=/content1/jane (accessed 16 September 2011).

_____. "Jane's Sentinel Security Assessment, Executive Summary, Jordan at a Glance." Armed Forces, Jordan. http://sentinel.janes.com/subscribe/sentinel/doc_view_print.jsp?K2DocKey=/content1/janes (accessed 16 September 2011).

_____. "Jane's World Armies-Bahrain." http://jwar.janes.com/subscribe/jwar/doc_view_print.jsp?K2DocKey=content1/janesdata/bi (accessed 4 February 2012).

_____. "Jane's World Armies–Jordan." http://jwar.janes.com/subscribe/jwar/doc_view_print.jsp?K2DocKey=content1/janesdata/bi (accessed 16 September 2011, 2 February 2012, and 4 February 2012).

_____. "Jane's World Armies-Kingdom of Saudi Arabia." http://jwar.janes.com/subscribe/jwar/doc_view_print.jsp?K2DocKey=content1/janesdata/bi (accessed 4 February 2012).

_____. Jane's World Armies-Kuwait." http://jwar.janes.com/subscribe/jwar/doc_view_print.jsp?K2DocKey=content1/janesdata/bi (accessed 4 February 2012).

_____. "Jane's World Armies-Morocco." http://jwar.janes.com/subscribe/jwar/doc_view_print.jsp?K2DocKey=/content1/janesdata/bi (accessed 4 February 2012).

_____. "Jane's World Armies-Oman." http://jwar.janes.com/subscribe/jwar/doc_view_print.jsp?K2DocKey=content1/janesdata/bi (accessed 4 February 2012).

_____. "Jane's World Armies–United Arab Emirates." http://jwar.janes.com/subscribe/jwar/doc_view_print.jsp?K2DocKey=/content1/janesdata/bi (accessed 4 Febraury 2012).

_____. "Jane's World Armies-Qatar." http://jwar.janes.com/subscribe/jward/doc_view_print.jsp?K2DocKey=/content1/janesdata/bi (accessed 4 February 2012).

"Jordan–Constitution." http://www.kinghussein.gov.jo/const_ch1-9.html (accessed 16 April 2012),

Kermali, Shenaz. "The GCC is Expanding its Army, but for What?" Aljazeera.net. http://english.aljazeera.net/indepth/features/2011/06/20116262649845386.html (accessed 8 November 2011).

"Kuwait–Constitution." http://www.servat.unibe.ch/icl/ku00000_.html (accessed 25 March 2012).

Library of Congress. "Country Studies." http://lcweb2.loc.gov/cgi-bin/query/r?frd/cstdy:@field(DOCID+qa0070) (accessed 20 March 2012).

McDonnell, Patrick J. "Los Angeles Times Online." *Los Angeles Times.* http://latimes blogs.latimes.com/world_now/2011/11/syria-arab-league-suspension.html (accessed 3 April 2012).

Mekhennet, Souad. "Bahrain Women Take Pride in Vital Protest Role." *New York Times,* 21 December 2011. http://www.nytimes.com/2011/12/21/world/middleeast/bahrain-women-take-pride-in-vital-protest-role (accessed 16 March 2012).

"Morocco–Constitution." http://www.al-bab.com/maroc/gov/con96.htm (accessed 16 April 2012).

"Oman–Constitution." http://www.servat.unibe.ch/icl/mu00000_.html (accessed 25 March 2012).

Patheos. "Religion Library:Sunni Islam." http://www.patheos.com/Library/Sunni-Islam.html (accessed 4 April 2012).

"Peninsula Shield Forces Enter Bahrain to Maintain Order." *Asharq Al Awsat Newspaper* (15 March 2011). http://www.asharq-e.com/news.asp?section=1&id=24509, (accessed 17 September 2011).

"Qatar–Constitution." http://www.qatarembassy.net/constitution.asp (accessed 19 March 2012).

Queenann, Gavriel. "Jordan to Join the GCC in September." Arutz Sheva, Israel National News. http://israelnationalnews.com/news.news.aspx/146512 (accessed 5 October 2011).

Richter, Fredrik, and Martina Fuchs. "Gulf Troops Staying until 'Iran' Threat Gone." *Jordan Times.* Reuters. http://www.jordantimes.com/?news=36659 (accessed 8 September 2011).

Sajedi, Sayyed Mohiyeddin. "[P]GCC Overturns Membership Invitations." Iranian PressTV. http://www.presstv.ir/detail/213784.html.

"Saudi Arabia–Constitution." http://www.servate.unibe.ch/icl/sa00000_.html (accessed 15 March 2012).

Saudi Press Agency. "Saudi Arabia Opens New Facility for Peninsula Shield Force." Saudi News Agency. http://lumen.cgsccarl.com/login?url=http://proquest.umi. com/pqdweb?did=472048591&Fmt=3&clientId=5094&RQT=309&VName=PQ D (accessed 16 November 2011).

Schenker, David. "The Cutting Edge." The Washington Institute. http://www.the cuttingedgenews.com/index.php?article=52902&pageid=&pagename= (accessed 6 April 2012).

Shanker, Thom, and Steven Lee Myers. "U.S. Planning Troop Buildup in Gulf after Exit from Iraq." *New York Times,* 30 October 2011. http://www.nytimes.com/ 2011/10/30/world/middleeast/united-states-plans-post-iraq-troop-increase-in-persian-gulf.html?_r=1&pagewanted=all (accessed 3 January 2012).

Staff Writers. "Arabs Plan $63 Billion Air Power Buildup." United Press International. http://www.spacewar.com/reports/Arab_plan_63_billion_air _power_ buildup_999.html (accessed 4 October 2011).

Sweney, Mark. "Al-Jazeera Office Attacked in Egypt Protests." *The Guardian.* http://www.guardian.co.uk/media/2011/feb/04/al-jazeera-office-attack (accessed 2 April 2012).

"United Arab Emirates–Constitution." http://www.uaecabinet.ae/English/UAE Government/Pages/constitution_1_1.aspx, (accessed 25 March 2012).

Tawazun Holdings. "Military and Sporting Weapons." Tawazun. http://www.tawazun. ae/en/our-subsidiaries/military-and-sporting-weapons.aspx (accessed 17 April 2012).

United Nations. "UN at a Glance." http://www.un.org/en/aboutun/index.shtml (accessed 4 February 2012).

The World Bank Group. "Countries and Economies." http://data.worldbank.org/country (accessed 4 February 2012).

Papers/Theses/Dissertations

Kuffel, Glenn P. Jr. "The Gulf Cooperation Council's Peninsula Shield Force." Naval War College, Newport, RI, 2000.

McKnight, Sean, Neil Partrick, and Francis Toase. "Gulf Security: Opportunities and Challenges for the New Generation." London, RUSI Whitehall Paper Series, 2000.

Terrill, W. Andrew. "Kuwaiti National Security and The U.S.-Kuwaiti Strategic Relationship After Saddam." Carlisle, PA: Strategic Studies Institute, 2007.

Journals/Periodicals

Al-Saeri, Muqbil. "A Talk with Peninsula Shield Force Commander Mutlaq Bin Salem Al-Azima." *Asharq Alawsat* (28 March 2011).

Belfer, Mitchell A. "The Fourteenth Province: The Irano-Bahrain Conflict in Perspective." *Central European Journal of International and Security Studies* (2011): 5, 7.

Eakin, Hugh. "The Strange Power of Qatar." *New York Review* (27 October 2011): 43.

Other Sources

Gastaldo, Andrea. Personal experience as an officer within the U.S. Embassy living under Saudi regulations while assigned to Riyadh, 1998-2000.

_____. Personal experience during the brief succession crisis in Kuwait, January 2006.